Cambridge Elements

Elements in Epistemology
edited by
Stephen Hetherington
University of New South Wales, Sydney

RELIABILISM AND ITS RIVALS

Bob Beddor
*University of Florida and
University of Johannesburg*

CAMBRIDGE
UNIVERSITY PRESS

Shaftesbury Road, Cambridge CB2 8EA, United Kingdom

One Liberty Plaza, 20th Floor, New York, NY 10006, USA

477 Williamstown Road, Port Melbourne, VIC 3207, Australia

314–321, 3rd Floor, Plot 3, Splendor Forum, Jasola District Centre,
New Delhi – 110025, India

103 Penang Road, #05–06/07, Visioncrest Commercial, Singapore 238467

Cambridge University Press is part of Cambridge University Press & Assessment,
a department of the University of Cambridge.

We share the University's mission to contribute to society through the pursuit of
education, learning and research at the highest international levels of excellence.

www.cambridge.org
Information on this title: www.cambridge.org/9781009645454

DOI: 10.1017/9781009645485

© Bob Beddor 2025

This publication is in copyright. Subject to statutory exception and to the provisions
of relevant collective licensing agreements, no reproduction of any part may take
place without the written permission of Cambridge University Press & Assessment.

When citing this work, please include a reference to the DOI 10.1017/9781009645485

First published 2025

A catalogue record for this publication is available from the British Library

ISBN 978-1-009-64545-4 Hardback
ISBN 978-1-009-64549-2 Paperback
ISSN 2398-0567 (online)
ISSN 2514-3832 (print)

Cambridge University Press & Assessment has no responsibility for the persistence
or accuracy of URLs for external or third-party internet websites referred to in this
publication and does not guarantee that any content on such websites is, or will remain,
accurate or appropriate.

For EU product safety concerns, contact us at Calle de José Abascal, 56, 1°, 28003
Madrid, Spain, or email eugpsr@cambridge.org

Reliabilism and Its Rivals

Elements in Epistemology

DOI: 10.1017/9781009645485
First published online: December 2025

Bob Beddor
*University of Florida and
University of Johannesburg*

Author for correspondence: Bob Beddor, rbeddor@gmail.com

Abstract: According to reliabilism, whether a belief is justified is a matter of whether it was reliably formed. Reliabilism is one of the leading theories of justification, and it holds important explanatory advantages: It sheds light on the connection between justification and truth, and it offers to situate justification within a naturalistic worldview. However, reliabilism faces well-known problems. One promising strategy for overcoming these problems is to modify reliabilism, combining it with elements of views that have been traditionally regarded as rivals, such as evidentialism. This Element offers an opinionated survey of the prospects for reliabilist epistemology, paying particular attention to recent reliabilist-evidentialist hybrid views.

Keywords: reliabilism, justification, evidence, truth, knowledge

© Bob Beddor 2025

ISBNs: 9781009645454 (HB), 9781009645492 (PB), 9781009645485 (OC)
ISSNs: 2398-0567 (online), 2514-3832 (print)

Contents

	Introduction: What This Element Is About	1
1	Reliabilism, A Primer	2
2	The Appeal of Reliabilism	10
3	Headaches for Reliabilists	18
4	Evidence to the Rescue?	43
5	Toward a More Promising Reliabilist Epistemology	54
	Conclusion	71
	References	73

Introduction: What This Element Is About

We have many beliefs. Some are justified. Consider scientific beliefs that are formed after carefully consulting the available evidence and ruling out alternative hypotheses, or perceptual beliefs about nearby objects formed in good lighting conditions, or your clear recollections of what you had for breakfast this morning.

Other beliefs are not justified. Consider beliefs formed *via* wishful thinking, or beliefs tainted by bias, or beliefs formed from shoddy guesswork.

It's easy enough to list some paradigmatic examples of justified and unjustified beliefs. Can we say anything more systematic about the distinction? That is, can we give a general account of what makes a belief justified or unjustified?

This question has received a tremendous amount of attention from epistemologists. There are at least two reasons why epistemologists have been so interested in justification. First, justification matters to us. We want our beliefs to be justified. Second, many epistemologists have held that justification is closely connected with other epistemic statuses, for example, knowledge. Someone who merely believes, for no good reason, that there is an even number of stars in the universe and happens to get this right does not *know* that there is an even number of stars. This has suggested to some epistemologists that justification is a necessary condition on knowledge. If this is right, then insofar as epistemologists are interested in understanding knowledge, they should also be interested in understanding justification.

This Element is about how to understand justification. Specifically, it is about one prominent theory of justification: *reliabilism*. The key idea behind reliabilism is that justification is closely connected to reliability:

> *Core Reliabilist Idea:* Whether a belief is justified is largely a matter of whether it is reliably formed.

Reliabilism is a controversial view. Some of the controversies are in-house: There are disagreements among reliabilists about how to understand the sort of reliability required for justification. The more significant controversies concern whether we should buy into the core reliabilist idea in the first place. Why think reliability has anything to do with justification?

The aim of this Element is to explore these controversies and make progress toward resolving them. I start (Section 1) by explaining reliabilism in more detail. I proceed (Section 2) to highlight some selling points of reliabilism. These include its ability to capture our intuitive judgments about paradigm cases of justified and unjustified beliefs, its response to skepticism, and its ability to situate epistemic properties within a naturalistic worldview. These selling points go some way to answering the question: Why think justification has anything to do with reliability?

After the good news comes the bad. Section 3 reviews some problems facing reliabilism. Philosophers have objected that reliability is not necessary for justification (Section 3.1), that it is not sufficient for justification (Sections 3.2 and 3.3), and also that the very idea of a reliably formed belief cannot be articulated with sufficient precision (Section 3.4). These problems have convinced some philosophers that reliabilism must be abandoned.

While these philosophers do not always agree on what should take its place, one popular alternative is *evidentialism*. The key idea behind evidentialism is that justification is closely tied to evidence:

> *Core Evidentialist Idea:* Whether a belief is justified is largely a matter of whether it is supported by the believer's evidence.

But should we abandon reliabilism so readily? Not so fast, say I. Reliabilism has significant explanatory advantages, and evidentialism faces problems of its own. This raises an interesting prospect. Perhaps some view that synthesizes elements of reliabilism with aspects of evidentialism could offer the best of both worlds, retaining the advantages of reliabilism while also avoiding its problems.

The second half of the Element is devoted to exploring this prospect: I examine in detail different ways of synthesizing reliabilism with evidentialism. We'll see (Section 4) that many extant attempts to wed reliabilism with evidentialism face important difficulties: They either fail to fully solve the problems for reliabilism, or they abandon the very features that rendered reliabilism attractive. In Section 5, I sketch two paths toward developing a more promising synthesis – a synthesis that retains the virtues of both views while avoiding the most pressing worries.

What is my overall message about reliabilism? Is the view correct? My answer will not be one of unqualified endorsement, but one of cautious optimism. The advantages of reliabilism should not be abandoned lightly. Moreover, some of the problems for reliabilism arose because of some specific – and ultimately dispensable – features of early formulations of reliabilism. A view that retains reliabilist commitment while adopting a somewhat different structure (in particular, taking on board evidentialist elements) offers a promising path forward.

1 Reliabilism, A Primer

1.1 Process Reliabilism Introduced

The key reliabilist idea is that justification is a matter of reliability: A belief is justified provided it is reliably formed. But what does this mean? The most common answer spells this out in terms of the reliability of the *process* through which the belief was formed and sustained. This theory is known as "process reliabilism." In its simplest version:

> *Simple Process Reliabilism:* A belief is justified iff it is produced by a reliable belief-forming process.

Process reliabilism has been developed in most detail by Alvin Goldman (see esp. Goldman 1979, 1986, 2012), though other epistemologists have also made important contributions to process reliabilism.[1] Perhaps the earliest explicit formulation of a reliabilist theory, due to Ramsey (1931), also appealed to the reliability of the belief-forming process (though Ramsey's view was proposed as a theory of knowledge rather than justification).

How should we understand the notion of a belief-forming process? The background thought is that different cognitive processes are responsible for different beliefs. Compare my current perceptual belief that there is a dog outside my window with my recollection that I ate foie gras for breakfast this morning. If asked to describe the process responsible for the former belief, a natural answer would be *vision*. If asked to name the process responsible for the latter belief, a natural answer would be *memory*. For process reliabilists, the key idea is that the justificatory status of the belief depends on the reliability of the process that caused it. If my vision is reliable, then my resulting belief that there is a dog outside my window is justified.

Now, there are tricky issues about how to describe the relevant belief-forming processes. For example, why describe the process responsible for my belief about the dog as *vision*, rather than *vision of a dog,* or *vision of an animate creature formed in good lighting conditions on a Tuesday afternoon*? This turns out to be one of the main challenges to reliabilism: the "Generality Problem." We'll discuss this issue in detail in Section 3.4.

Process reliabilism is not the only reliabilist theory of justification.[2] But it is the most well-developed and prominent reliabilist theory of justification. For this reason, it will serve as our primary focus, though I will highlight differences with other reliabilist theories when they prove relevant.

---

[1] See Kornblith (2002), Lyons (2009), among others. Goldman's original 1979 formulation of reliabilism was somewhat more complicated than the simple version. It took a recursive structure, and introduced complications to handle cases of defeat. Goldman also explored numerous revisions to his views in later works (e.g., Goldman 1986, 2011a). For the purposes of clarity and accessibility, I will start by focusing on Simple Process Reliabilism, only introducing complications as they become relevant.

[2] Another reliabilist theory of justification is indicator reliabilism, which holds that a belief is justified if it is based on grounds that reliably indicate the truth (Alston 1998, 2005; Tang 2016). I return to Tang's view in Section 5. For a general overview of various forms of reliabilism, see Goldman and Beddor (2021).

1.2 What Is Reliability?

What does it mean for a process to be "reliable"? Typically, reliabilists hold that a process is reliable if it tends to produce true beliefs rather than false beliefs (Goldman 1979, 1986; Lyons 2009). The underlying thought is that we can define reliability in terms of a regular tendency to produce *successful* outputs. For example, a reliable vending machine tends to successfully deliver whatever item one has selected. Similarly, a reliable belief-forming process usually produces successful beliefs rather than unsuccessful beliefs. This is then combined with the idea that truth is the epistemic success condition for belief: A belief is successful, from the epistemic point of view, if and only if it is true.[3]

How should we understand a *tendency* to produce true beliefs? Perhaps the most common understanding is that a process tends to produce true beliefs if it produces a high ratio of true to false beliefs in some relevant domain of situations (Goldman 1979). This proposal calls for clarification on two fronts.

The first concerns how to define the relevant domain of situations. One option is to say that the relevant situations are those which are nearby to the world of the believer. Another is to say that the relevant situations are those where conditions are normal for the operation of the belief-forming process. We'll discuss these options – and some others – in more detail in Section 3.

On to the second point of clarification: How reliable does a process need to be? According to Goldman (1979), we should not expect a precise answer. Our ordinary concept of justification is vague. This is, Goldman thinks, not a problem for reliabilism: We should only expect precision in an analysis to the extent we find precision in the *analysandum* (the concept we are trying to analyze). Consider an analogy with other gradable adjectives, such as "tall" and "expensive." We should not expect an analysis of our ordinary concept *expensive* to deliver a precise cut-off for what counts as expensive.

1.3 Reliabilism about Justification v. Reliabilism about Knowledge

This Element will focus on reliabilism as a theory of *justified belief*. However, it is worth noting that some philosophers present reliabilism as a theory of *knowledge*. As previously noted, one of the earliest reliabilist proposals was due to Ramsey

---

[3] While this is certainly the most common way reliabilists conceive of epistemic success, it's not the only option. Kelp (2016) defends a view on which the epistemic success condition for belief is *knowledge*. This could then be plugged into the process reliabilist schema, yielding a view on which an agent's belief is justified if and only if it was produced by a process that tends to produce knowledge, not merely true belief. See Simion (2019) for a related proposal.

(1931), who proposed that a belief amounts to knowledge if it is true, certain, and reliably formed.

Several other theories of knowledge have strong reliabilist affinities. For example, Goldman's (1967) causal theory of knowing held that A knows p if and only if there is an appropriate causal connection between the fact that p and A's belief that p. This view has clear reliabilist elements. Specifically, the emphasis on the causal processes responsible for the belief is a key feature of reliabilism (more on this later).

Or consider so-called "truth-tracking" theories of knowledge. The basic idea behind these theories is that a belief amounts to knowledge if it reliably *tracks the truth*. To illustrate with an analogy from Feldman (2002), consider a thermometer that is perfectly reliable. Part of what this means is that if it is 98 degrees outside, the thermometer will read "98." Moreover, if it were **not** 98 degrees outside, the thermometer would not read "98." In such circumstances, we might be willing to say the thermometer "knows" the temperature. According to truth-tracking theories, this metaphorical knowledge is pretty much the way real knowledge works: knowledge involves having beliefs that reliably track facts in the world.[4]

There are different ways of spelling out the relevant sense of "tracking." Nozick (1981) developed this idea in terms of a condition he called "sensitivity":

> *Sensitivity:* Suppose A believes p using method X. Then A's belief amounts to knowledge only if in the nearest possible worlds where p is false and A uses X to arrive at a belief about whether p is true, A does not believe p.[5]

For example, suppose I look out of my window and come to know that there is a dog outside. According to sensitivity, this requires that in all the most similar scenarios where there is not a dog outside but I still look out of my window, I do not come to (falsely) believe that there is a dog outside. (See Figure 1.)

More recently, some epistemologists have proposed a slightly different truth-tracking condition, called "safety":

> *Safety:* Suppose A believes p using method X. Then A's belief amounts to knowledge only if in the nearest possible worlds where A believes p using X, p is true.[6]

---

[4] Armstrong (1973) also relies on an analogy with a thermometer in developing a reliabilist theory of knowledge.
[5] Nozick also proposed an "adherence" condition, which requires that in the nearest worlds where p is true and one forms a belief using X, one believes p.
[6] See for example, Sosa (1999), Williamson (2000), Pritchard (2005), and Lasonen-Aarnio (2010). A variant formulation of safety appeals to truth in worlds that are at least as normal as those the believer inhabits (Beddor and Pavese 2020). More on this in Section 3.

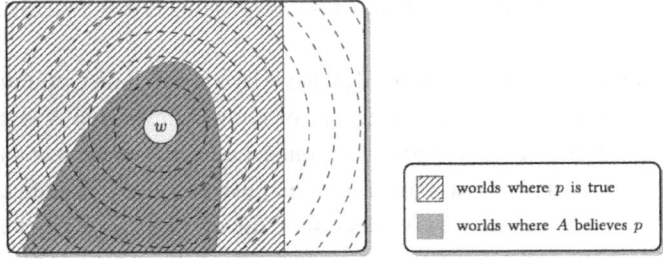

Figure 1 A sensitive belief. (At none of the nearest worlds to w where p is false is p believed.)

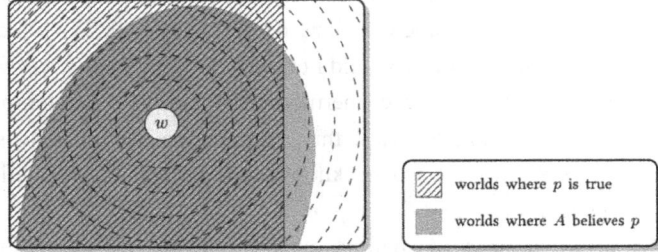

Figure 2 A safe but insensitive belief. (At all the nearest worlds to w where p is believed, p is true. But at the nearest worlds where p is false, p is still believed.)

To illustrate using the dog example: According to Safety, if I come to know that there is a dog outside my window, this means that in the most similar scenarios where I look out of my window and form the belief that there is a dog outside, my belief is true: There is a dog outside.

Both sensitivity and safety can be viewed as ways of articulating a reliabilist condition on knowledge. Both claim that knowledge involves reliably tracking the truth; they just differ in the range of scenarios across which reliability is required. Sensitivity focuses on scenarios where the relevant proposition is false: The question is whether the agent avoids believing a falsehood in those scenarios. Safety looks at nearby scenarios where the agent forms the same belief, asking whether the agent's belief is true in those scenarios. (See Figure 2.)[7]

---

[7] To see where sensitivity and safety come apart, consider a skeptical hypothesis, for example, you are just part of a computer simulation. Presumably, you believe this skeptical hypothesis is false. According to sensitivity, this belief does not amount to knowledge, since in the nearest worlds where you are in a computer simulation, you still mistakenly believe that you are not in a computer simulation. But your belief could be safe: in the nearest worlds where you believe

How do these proposals relate to process reliabilism? There are clear similarities. Both sensitivity and safety assign an important role to the *method* responsible for the belief, which seems roughly the same as the *process* which caused the belief (talk of "methods" and "processes" seems interchangeable). But unlike process reliabilism, sensitivity and safety are factive conditions: If a belief is either sensitive or safe, it follows that it is true. By contrast, most process reliabilists want to allow that reliability is compatible with error. Most hold that the threshold for reliability is not 100 percent, so a belief can be reliably formed yet still false. This difference can be traced to the different properties of knowledge and justification. Knowledge is factive: If a belief amounts to knowledge, it is true. By contrast, most philosophers have thought that it's possible to have justified false beliefs.

This difference illustrates a more general point. We should expect some differences between a reliabilist condition on knowledge and a reliabilist condition on justification, given the important differences between knowledge and justification.

1.4 The Revolutionary Nature of Reliabilism

By now, "reliabilism" is part of our shared philosophical vocabulary. But when it was first introduced, reliabilism was a revolutionary idea. Indeed, much of the ongoing resistance to reliabilism stems from the radical nature of its central claims.

What makes reliabilism so radical? In retrospect, we can view reliabilism as a leading character in two closely related philosophical revolutions – what we might call the "externalist revolution" and the "causal revolution."

1.4.1 The Externalist Revolution

Historically, many philosophers have thought about justification in "internalist" terms. Roughly, they have sought to explain justification in terms of factors that are accessible to an individual's mind. A particularly clear version of this internalist orientation can be found in Descartes' *Meditations*. Descartes can be interpreted as posing a version of our starting question: Which beliefs are justified? To answer this question, he considers a series of skeptical possibilities designed to cast doubt on his beliefs. If he can discern no grounds for rejecting some skeptical hypothesis h, then he provisionally rejects any beliefs that are incompatible with h. Crucially, the grounds in

---

you are not in a computer simulation, this belief is true. (Figure 2 depicts a case with this structure.) We'll discuss how process reliabilism interacts with skepticism in the next section.

question are internalist grounds: They are sensory experiences or a priori considerations that are accessible to Descartes from his armchair.[8]

This internalist tradition also has many contemporary adherents. Consider evidentialism, the view that justification is a matter of evidential support. This view is often considered the main rival to reliabilism. (Though whether they are necessarily rivals can and should be questioned; indeed, this will be one of the major themes of this Element.) While there are different ways of articulating evidentialism, a common formulation goes like this:

> *Evidentialism:* Necessarily, S is epistemically justified in believing p at time t iff S's total evidence supports believing p at t.[9]

Evidentialism is not wedded to internalism. All depends on how we unpack the notions of evidence and evidential support. That said, most evidentialists have been internalists. For example, Conee and Feldman (2008) defend a picture on which an agent's ultimate evidence consists in their experiences. One possible motivation for this picture comes from the idea that we have privileged introspective access to our experiences. If justification is entirely a function of evidence, and evidence itself consists in mental states to which we have armchair access, then justification depends entirely on facts that are accessible to us – or so the thought goes.[10]

Reliabilism marks a sharp break with this internalist tradition. According to reliabilism, the ultimate grounds for justification are facts about the reliability of our belief-forming processes. Whether a belief-forming process is reliable is typically not something that will be accessible to the believer from the armchair. This is because whether a process is reliable typically depends on contingent facts about what the world is like. For example, vision is typically a reliable way of forming beliefs about objects in one's immediate surroundings. But suppose

---

[8] Internalism was also a shared commitment of the empiricist tradition stretching from Locke, Berkeley, and Hume through the logical empiricists. A central goal of this tradition was to figure out which of our beliefs about the world can be rationally inferred from our sensory experiences, together with any a priori certainties to which we are privy (if any there be).

[9] See for example, Conee and Feldman (2004) and McCain (2014).

[10] Some distinguish between two versions of internalism: *accessibilism* and *mentalism* (e.g., Feldman and Conee 2001). Accessibilists hold that justification only depends on factors that are accessible to the agent. Mentalists hold that justification only depends on the agent's mental states. Given this taxonomy, there is room to be a mentalist internalist without being an accessibilist. However, in practice most mentalist internalists take justification to depend only on a privileged subset of our mental states, such as our *experiences* or our *seemings*. This privileged subset seems to be the very mental states that, according to historical tradition, are directly accessible to the agent. This suggests that many internalist mentalists are often motivated (perhaps implicitly) by considerations of accessibility. See Smithies (2014) for relevant discussion.

we lived in a world where optical illusions and mirages were commonplace. In such a world, vision would be unreliable.

This aspect of reliabilism has a surprising and – in the eyes of some – disconcerting consequence: There is an element of luck in whether we are justified in believing something. Two people can be alike "from the inside": They can have all the same experiences and phenomenal states, yet one of their beliefs is justified and the other not. This consequence forms the backbone of a major objection to reliabilism – the "new evil demon problem" (to be discussed in Section 3).

1.4.2 The Causal Revolution

Another distinctive feature of reliabilism is its emphasis on *causal* factors. For reliabilists, the justificatory status of a belief depends on the reliability of the process that *caused* that belief. Much of the internalist tradition described earlier focuses on the epistemologist's job as a constructive or ameliorative project: The aim of the game is to construct a new and improved positive rationale for our beliefs. This approach typically pays little attention to the question of what factors have caused ordinary people's beliefs. At least for Descartes, there was a presumption that whatever factors had causally sustained these beliefs in the past were epistemically inadequate, which is why a new philosophical rationale is needed. By contrast, reliabilism puts the causal question front and center.

In this regard, reliabilism can be viewed as part of a larger causal revolution that occurred in the mid twentieth century. This movement sought to analyze a variety of concepts in causal terms. Some examples:

Causal Theories of Perception. For an influential early example, consider Grice's causal theory of perception (Grice 1961). Suppose you go out celebrity-spotting in Hollywood and you see your favorite celebrity, Nicolas Cage. According to Grice, part of what is involved in seeing Nicolas Cage is for you to have a certain visual experience that is caused, in an appropriate way, by Nicolas Cage. If instead, your visual experience was caused by a Cage doppelganger, or by a Madame Tussaud's wax sculpture, then you did not *see* Nicolas Cage.[11]

Causal Theories of Content. Around the same time that process reliabilism was developed, various philosophers explored the idea that mental and semantic content can be explained in causal terms. Causal theories of content come in different forms. But to illustrate the basic idea, consider my concept of my next-door neighbor, Fred. According to causal approaches, part of what makes my

---

[11] In developing his causal theory of knowledge, Goldman cited the causal theory of perception as an inspiration (1967).

concept about Fred – rather than, say, about his identical twin, or someone else named "Fred" – is that I have causally interacted with Fred.[12]

Thus, reliabilism is a contribution to a multifaceted research program seeking to explain philosophical concepts in causal terms.

The causal aspect of reliabilism is closely tied to its *historical* dimension. The factors that caused a belief are part of its history. Consequently, reliabilists hold that the history of a belief determines whether that belief is justified. Process reliabilism thus stands opposed to current "time-slice" theories, which maintain that the justificatory status of a belief at time t is entirely a function of facts that obtain at time t.[13]

Having articulated some key reliabilist concepts, I now turn to consider why many philosophers have found reliabilism an attractive view.

2 The Appeal of Reliabilism

Why think justification has anything to do with reliability? This section highlights some reasons for finding reliabilism attractive. Along the way, I discuss whether rival theories – such as internalist evidentialism – can claim the same advantages.

2.1 Capturing Paradigm Cases

An initial motivation for reliabilism is its ability to capture paradigm cases of justified and unjustified beliefs. Consider: What are some processes that typically cause *un*justified beliefs? Goldman answers:

> Here are some examples: confused reasoning, wishful thinking, reliance on emotional attachment, mere hunchwork or guesswork, and hasty generalization. What do these faulty processes have in common? They share the feature of *unreliability*: they tend to produce *error* a large proportion of the time. (1979: 95)

What are some processes that typically yield justified beliefs? Goldman answers:

> They include standard perceptual processes, remembering, good reasoning, and introspection. What these processes seem to have in common is *reliability*: the beliefs they produce are generally true. (1979: 95)

Goldman's observations strike me as correct. Many paradigm instances of epistemically "good" (justification-conferring) processes are reliable, and

---

[12] See Stampe (1977), Dretske (1981), Fodor (1987), among many others.
[13] See Goldman (1979: 98). In his original formulation of process reliabilism, Goldman emphasized this feature, referring to his view as "Historical Reliabilism." For recent defenses of time-slice epistemology, see Moss (2015), Hedden (2015), for pushback, see Podgorski (2017).

similarly, many paradigm instances of epistemically "bad" (unjustified belief-producing) processes are unreliable.

While this point is suggestive, as an argument for reliabilism it has two limitations. First, there might be other properties besides reliability that "good" processes have in common. Evidentialists will stress that Goldman's examples of good processes also typically result in *evidentially supported* beliefs. Similarly, Goldman's examples of bad processes typically result in beliefs that are *not* evidentially supported. Evidentialists may claim that our intuitions are being driven by the presence or absence of evidential support rather than reliability. Second, it is not obvious that *all* beliefs resulting from reliable processes are intuitively justified, or that *all* beliefs resulting from unreliable processes are intuitively unjustified. Many of the putative counter-examples to reliabilism purport to show that this is not the case (more on this in the next section).

2.2 The Truth Connection

Another argument for reliabilism is more theoretical. Reliabilism captures the idea that there is an important connection between justification and truth.

We care about having true beliefs. That is:

> *Truth Goal:* All else equal, we want to have true beliefs and to avoid having false beliefs.[14]

We also care about having justified beliefs. As noted in the Introduction:

> *Justification Goal:* All else equal, we want to have justified beliefs, and to avoid having unjustified beliefs.

What is the connection between the Truth Goal and the Justification Goal? Are these just completely separate things we happen to care about from the epistemic point of view? Such a disconnect seems both implausible and theoretically dissatisfying. Surely there is some unifying thread explaining why both truth and justification are epistemically valuable.

Reliabilism offers a way of drawing this connection. Justified beliefs are truth-conducive: They are formed in a manner that tends to yield the truth. So achieving the Justification Goal is conducive to attaining the Truth Goal.[15]

---

[14] We could also frame this point in terms of value: true beliefs are epistemically valuable. Some philosophers go a step further, arguing that true belief is the only thing that is ultimately (i.e., non-derivatively) epistemically valuable – a position known as "veritism."

[15] Reliabilism is compatible with the veritist view (mentioned in the previous footnote) that the only thing that is ultimately epistemically valuable is true belief. On this view, justified belief is only derivatively valuable; its epistemic value is explained entirely in terms of the fact that justification is conducive to the goal of truth.

This is a selling point, to be sure. But is this selling point unique to reliabilism? Consider evidentialism. As we will see shortly, many evidentialists explain evidential support in probabilistic terms: A belief is supported by the evidence if it is likely to be true, given the evidence. Evidentialists might claim that this secures a connection between justification and truth: If someone achieves the Justification Goal, their belief is likely to be true, given their evidence.

This is right, as far as it goes. But exactly what sort of connection the evidentialist establishes between justification and truth depends on how we understand *evidential probability*. As we have seen, many evidentialists understand evidence and evidential support in purely internalist terms. Consequently, a person's belief can satisfy the (internalist) evidentialist's condition even if their belief is *anti*-reliable – that is, it is formed in a manner that leads to falsehood far more frequently than truth. By the reliabilist's lights, this calls into question whether this provides a sufficiently robust connection between justification and truth to be worth caring about. This marks one of the major divisions between reliabilists and internalists.[16]

2.3 Naturalistic Reduction

2.3.1 Reliabilism's Reductive Ambitions

Another motivation for reliabilism is its naturalistic payoff. Reliabilism explains justification using non-epistemic, naturalistic concepts. This motivation played a prominent role in Goldman's 1979 paper, where he declares, "I want a theory of justified belief to specify in non-epistemic terms when a belief is justified" (90). To introduce some helpful terminology, let us call a theory "naturalistically reductive" if it satisfies this goal – that is, if it explains justification without recourse to any epistemic concepts.

What is an "epistemic" concept? It is hard to give a precise account of the epistemic/non-epistemic divide. But, very roughly, epistemic terms are those studied by epistemologists, for example, "knows," "has evidence that," "is rational in believing," and so on. For reliabilists, justification is a matter of reliability. Reliability is a non-epistemic notion: It is a matter of tending to produce true beliefs.[17]

---

[16] There are other externalist theories besides reliabilism. Some of these posit an even stronger connection between justification and truth. For example, some epistemologists have argued for the surprising view that justification requires knowledge (e.g., Sutton 2007; Williamson forthcoming). By contrast, most reliabilists regard it as a desideratum on a theory of justification that it allows for justified false beliefs.

[17] As noted in Section 1, standard reliabilism takes epistemic "success" to be a matter of achieving true belief. As we noted there, another option is to understand epistemic success as knowledge.

Why hanker after a reductive theory? Consider examples of successful reduction in science: say, the reduction of temperature to average kinetic energy, or the reduction of chemical properties to atomic physics. These are widely regarded as great achievements. They are great achievements, at least in part, because they enable us to see how different parts of the world fit together. Chemical properties do not "float free" of the underlying atomic properties. By reducing the former to the latter, we integrated the two into a unified worldview. Naturalists in epistemology have a similar goal. Epistemic properties do not float free from non-epistemic properties; the former depend on the latter. A naturalistically reductive view would allow us to see how epistemic properties fit into the natural world.

2.3.2 Comparison with Evidentialism

This marks a potential advantage of reliabilism over evidentialism. Evidentialists explain justification in further epistemic terms – namely, whether an agent's evidence supports believing some proposition.

Closer examination reveals that evidentialists rely on two epistemic notions in their analysis. First, evidentialists explain justification in terms of the believer's evidence – that is, the evidence that the believer *possesses*. Second, evidentialists say that justification is a function of whether someone's (possessed) evidence *supports* believing some proposition. So evidentialists invoke two epistemic notions: (i) the notion of *possessing* some evidence *e*; and (ii) the notion of *e supporting* some belief.

Of course, there is nothing to stop evidentialists from providing a naturalistic reduction of these notions. But the devil is in the details. And spelling out these devilish details is harder than has been traditionally recognized. So it is worth taking a brief excursion into the evidentialist's options and seeing what obstacles arise. (Readers uninterested in the nuts and bolts of evidentialism's reductive prospects should feel free to skip ahead to Section 2.4.)

2.3.3 Explaining Evidence Possession

According to one influential version of evidentialism, an agent's evidence at time t consists in some of their mental states at t. On the face of it, this would seem to be a purely naturalistic approach of evidence possession: There does not seem to be anything inherently epistemic about the notion of being in some mental state. However, things are not so simple. Complications arise when we

---

Reliabilists who go this route have a less straightforward claim to providing a reductive theory: *knowledge* is an epistemic notion.

ask: Which mental states make the cut? Presumably not all of them. Suppose someone has a memory that is so deeply repressed that it would take years of extensive therapy to unearth. Most evidentialists would not want to consider this memory part of the agent's evidence (McCain 2014: 35). This is particularly true of internalist evidentialists who claim that justification depends only on features of the agent's mental life that are accessible to them.

Partly for this reason, many evidentialists have identified an agent's evidence with a particular subset of their mental states: Their *experiences* or their *seemings* (i.e., the way things seem to them).[18] But does this restriction solve the problem? It's doubtful that we always enjoy untrammeled access to our own experiences. I might experience a mild feeling of envy toward a colleague's success without being in a position to recognize that my experience is one of *envy*. Even if we restrict ourselves to still further to *perceptual* experiences or seemings, the problem persists. To take an example from Chisholm (1942): I might have a fleeting experience of a speckled hen, without having access to the exact number of speckles. In a similar vein, Schwitzgebel (2008) reports a range of empirical studies indicating that people are frequently mistaken about certain aspects of their perceptual experiences (e.g., the extent of their visual field). Thus insofar as evidentialists want to maintain an accessibility constraint on evidence, they should deny that all of an agent A's experiences – even all of A's perceptual experiences – comprise A's evidence.

Could evidentialists avoid the problem by just defining evidence in terms of accessibility? One might propose that an agent's evidence at time t is whatever mental states (or experiences specifically) the agent can access at t. The worry with this move is that "accessibility" appears to be an epistemically loaded notion. For a mental state to be accessible, in the relevant sense, is for the agent to be in a position to justifiably believe (or rationally believe, or know) that they are in that state. So if we define evidence in terms of accessibility, the resulting account of justification will not be naturalistically reductive. Worse, if the notion of accessibility is defined in terms of "justification" specifically, then the resulting account will be circular: We will have defined justification in terms of evidence, which is in turn defined in terms of justification.[19]

---

[18] For example, Conee and Feldman (2008) allow that while some beliefs qualify as evidence, they only do so derivatively. All "ultimate" evidence – that is, all evidence that does not derive from some further evidence – consists in experiences (2008: 88). Similar ideas have been defended in Lewis (1996) and Schroeder (2011).

[19] For development of the circularity worry for evidentialists, see Goldman (2011a) and Beddor (2015b). As noted above, not all evidentialists are internalists. For example, Williamson (2000) defends the view that E = K: someone possesses p as evidence iff they know p. Williamson combines this with the view that knowledge is "first"; it is not to be analyzed in terms of other epistemic notions, including justification. The resulting package of views is not circular: justification is explained in terms of evidence, which is explained in terms of knowledge,

This is not to suggest that evidentialists have no other resources available. From the perspective of this Element, one attractive strategy would be to explain accessibility in terms of *reliability*. For example, one might identify an agent's evidence as those mental states which the agent can reliably form beliefs about, or which serve as the inputs to their reliable processes. I explore such ideas in more detail in Section 5. For now, the important point is that any such move would mark a big departure from a "pure" internalist evidentialism, and a major step toward the reliabilist camp.

2.3.4 Explaining Evidential Support

Even if the evidentialist can unpack *evidence possession* in non-epistemic terms, there remains the question:

> *Evidential Support Question:* How should we understand evidential support? What does it take for evidence e to support believing p?

One common way of explaining evidential support is probabilistic. According to probabilistic views, e provides some support for a proposition p just in case it raises the probability of p:

> *Support as Probability-Raising:* Evidence e supports p iff $Pr(p|e) > Pr(p)$.

Evidentialists might suggest an agent's possessed evidence supports a belief just in case it boosts the probability of this belief's content above some threshold:

> *Probabilistic Account of Belief Support:* Evidence e supports believing p iff $Pr(p|e) > t$, where t is some threshold.

But how should we understand the probability function involved?

One approach says that *Pr* represents the subjective degrees of belief, also known as credences, of the agent. For subjective Bayesians, there are no constraints on these credences save internal coherence requirements (specifically, the requirement that the agent's credences obey the probability axioms) and the diachronic requirement to update by conditionalizing on one's total evidence. Credences are psychological states, which presumably can be understood in non-epistemic terms. So this approach is naturalistically reductive. But it is too permissive. To take an example from Greco (2013), suppose an agent starts off assigning credence 1 to the proposition that space invaders are lurking in our midst, and that to protect ourselves, we need to wear tin hats. Then for any evidence the agent gets that is logically consistent with this proposition, the

---

which is not explained in terms of justification. But this package of views is also not naturalistically reductive: knowledge is a paradigmatic epistemic notion.

probability of this proposition conditional on the agent's evidence will be 1. But it seems absurd to say that this agent's evidence supports believing this proposition, or that their resulting belief is *justified*.

This suggests that *Pr* cannot be any old credence function. Rather, *Pr* must represent epistemically *rational* or *justified* credences. But then we've just pushed our question back a step: How can we explain what it is for a credence to be epistemically rational or justified in non-epistemic terms?[20]

This is not to suggest that no answer can be provided. Here too, we might try to answer this question using reliabilist resources. I revisit this possibility in detail in Section 5.3.

2.4 Anti-Skeptical Payoff

2.4.1 Enter the Skeptic

Right now, the following seems to you to be true:

CHAIR: You are sitting in a chair, reading this book.

(Ok, I don't actually know if you seem to be sitting in a chair, but play along.)

Enter our old friend the skeptic. They start by spinning a yarn. You are not really sitting in your chair right now, reading a book. Rather, you are the victim of an evil demon, who has given you the illusion of sitting in a chair. Or you are a brain in a vat, plugged into a computer that is running a program designed to simulate your reading environment. Next, the skeptic claims that you cannot rule out the possibility that their tale is true. From this, they draw the conclusion that you cannot be *justified* in believing CHAIR.

2.4.2 Enter the Reliabilist

Reliabilism offers a straightforward response. According to process reliabilists, we need to ask: "What is the process responsible for your belief in CHAIR?" Presumably, the answer involves your visual and haptic senses. Next, we ask, "Are your senses reliable?" If, as a matter of fact, you are not in a skeptical scenario, the answer is plausibly *yes*. According to our common-sense understanding of the world, the senses typically yield true beliefs. If this common-sense conception of the world is correct, your belief in CHAIR is justified. The mere conceivability of vivid skeptical scenarios does not impugn the justificatory status of your beliefs.

---

[20] Not all evidentialists explain evidential support in probabilistic terms. Another option is to unpack evidential support in explanationist terms: roughly, *e* supports believing *p* iff the best explanation of *e* entails *p* (Conee and Feldman 2008: 97–98; McCain 2014: 172). One question for this approach is whether we can unpack what makes one explanation "best" in entirely non-epistemic terms. Another question is how this approach extends to degrees of belief.

Some find this reliabilist response unsatisfying. A natural reaction is to say, "But we can't tell whether our beliefs about the external world are produced by reliable processes! To assert that they are is to assume the very point at issue." This response – while initially tempting – faces two problems. The first is a dialectical point. The justificatory skeptic claims that justified beliefs about the external world are *impossible*: You cannot be justified in believing CHAIR regardless of what the world is like. That is, the justificatory skeptic says that even if the external world is exactly as common sense tells us, you still cannot be justified in your beliefs about the external world. The reliabilist shows how we can deny this. The reliabilist offers a possibility proof for justification: If both reliabilism and our common-sense understanding of the world are correct, then many of our beliefs about the external world are justified, contrary to what the skeptic claims.

Second, we should scrutinize the claim that we *cannot tell* whether our beliefs about the external world are produced by a genuinely reliable process. Here's something you also believe:

REL: My belief in CHAIR is justified.

What is the process responsible for your belief in REL? The answer may well be complex; it might involve, inter alia, your memory of your senses' past track record (e.g., that they tend not to lead you astray). Call whatever process is responsible for your belief in REL, 'P_{REL}.' Now, the reliabilist can make the same move as before: If P_{REL} is reliable, then your belief in REL is justified. If so, there is a real sense in which you *can* tell that your beliefs about the external world are produced by a reliable process. You can tell this in the sense that you can justifiably believe that they are so produced.

Admittedly, you cannot tell this in a way that is likely to convince the skeptic. You cannot point to any features of your experiences that prove that the skeptical hypothesis is false. But, according to reliabilists, providing such a proof is not required for justification. This is a key part of the externalist revolution.

2.4.3 Enter the Evidentialist

So the reliabilist offers a simple response to the skeptic. What does the evidentialist say? Here much depends on how we flesh out the details. As we saw, many evidentialists identify your evidence with certain experiences. And these experiences are often taken to include various appearances or seemings. They might thus think that your current evidence includes the proposition:

APPEARS: It appears that you are sitting in a chair, reading this book.

But how does this approach answer this skeptic? Why think that APPEARS supports believing CHAIR?

Evidentialists might point out that since CHAIR makes APPEARS very likely ($Pr(\text{APPEARS}|\text{CHAIR}) \cong 1$), and since we shouldn't in general expect to have appearances of sitting in chairs, it follows from Bayes' theorem that $Pr(\text{CHAIR}|\text{APPEARANCES}) > Pr(\text{CHAIR})$. Consequently, APPEARS provides at least *some* evidence for CHAIR. But this point does not get us very far. After all, compare CHAIR with the corresponding skeptical hypothesis:

DEMON-CHAIR: You are not really sitting in a chair, reading this book, but an evil demon is giving you the illusion of doing so.

By analogous reasoning, we can show that $Pr(\text{DEMON-CHAIR}|\text{APPEARS}) > Pr(\text{DEMON-CHAIR})$ – that is, the appearance of being in a chair provides *some* evidence that a demon is deceiving you into sitting in a chair.[21] So what is the basis for concluding that APPEARS favors CHAIR over DEMON-CHAIR?[22]

3 Headaches for Reliabilists

In the last section I painted a rosy picture of reliabilism, highlighting its explanatory virtues and advantages over rival theories. But not all is smooth sailing. Reliabilism faces a litany of challenges – challenges that have persuaded many epistemologists that reliabilism is untenable. This section reviews some of the most pressing challenges for reliabilists, along with some responses.

Here I focus on three types of challenges. First, challenges to the idea that reliability is *necessary* for justification; second, challenges to the idea that reliability is *sufficient* for justification; and third, challenges to the idea that there is a fact of the matter about which process is responsible for an agent's belief on a given occasion.

3.1 The New Evil Demon Problem

3.1.1 The Problem

The most famous objection to the idea that reliability is necessary for justification is the "New Evil Demon Problem" (Cohen 1984; see Graham forthcoming for a state-of-the-art discussion). Consider:

---

[21] See White (2006).

[22] One way evidentialists might respond is to adopt an externalist view of evidence. For example, Williamson (2000) defends a view that is nominally evidentialist, but identifies an agent's evidence with their knowledge. In a way, this gives an easy response to the skeptic: since you know CHAIR, the probability of CHAIR conditional on your evidence is 1, and so your evidence maximally supports believing CHAIR. But this response grants that justificatory facts do not supervene on facts that are internally accessible to the agent; consequently, it agrees with reliabilism in substantial respects. Moreover, insofar as one accepts a reliabilist condition on knowledge (as Williamson does), this view will not be an alternative to reliabilism.

Renée and the Demon. Renée's life seems perfectly ordinary. Alas, her perceptual experiences (and those of anyone else who inhabits her world) are caused by an evil demon hell-bent on deceiving Renée. When she seems to pick up her coffee cup in the morning, this is just a demon-induced illusion: there is no coffee cup in front of her. When she seems to scoop up her dog's poop on the walk, this is really ... Well, you get the picture.

A common intuition about this case is that Renée's perceptual beliefs are justified. For example, when she appears to see a tree in front of her, she is justified in believing that there is a tree in front of her. This poses a problem for reliabilism about justification.[23] At Renée's world, perception is systematically unreliable, thanks to the demon's machinations.

The New Evil Demon Problem is not just a problem for reliabilism. It threatens a wide variety of externalist views of justification. For example, it also poses a problem for hardline "knowledge first" views, according to which a belief is only justified if it amounts to knowledge.

Partly for this reason, some have regarded Renée and the Demon as a counterexample not just to reliabilism, but to any externalist theory. After all, the thought goes, the reason why we judge Renée to be justified is that her situation is internally indistinguishable from someone in the "good case" – that is, her counterpart who is not demonically deceived. And this, in turn, has suggested to some that justification supervenes on internally accessible states.

3.1.2 Bullet-Biting

One response is to deny that Renée is justified in holding her perceptual beliefs. Proponents of this response usually concede that Renée's beliefs have some positive epistemic status. But they deny that this status is the same as justification.

What is this positive status, if not justification? A couple of answers have been proposed.

Conditional Reliability. One answer, suggested by Lyons (2013), appeals to *conditional reliability*. Consider a process such as *believing the conjunction of your other beliefs*. Is this process reliable? Yes, if your other beliefs are true; no, if they are false. According to Goldman (1979) and Lyons (2013), we can evaluate a belief-dependent process along these lines (i.e., a process that takes other beliefs as input) for conditional reliability – that is, whether it typically delivers true outputs when it operates on true input beliefs.

---

[23] Emphasis on *justification*. Renée and the Demon is not a counterexample to reliabilist theories of knowledge. After all, knowledge is factive. Since Renée's perceptual beliefs are false, everyone should grant that they do not amount to knowledge.

Lyons (2013) suggests that there is a positive status associated with being the output of a conditionally reliable process, and that many of Renée's beliefs enjoy this status. Suppose Renée has various perceptual beliefs – she is drinking coffee, birds are chirping nearby – and from these beliefs she infers their conjunction. The belief in their conjunction was formed by a conditionally reliable belief-dependent process (conjunction introduction). Because of this, her conjunctive belief possesses a positive epistemic status, even though this status does not rise to the level of justification.[24]

Does this response solve the problem? Let me flag two worries. First, as Lyons recognizes, this response only delivers the conclusion that Renée's inferential beliefs have some positive epistemic status. But her non-inferential beliefs – which presumably include her basic perceptual beliefs – lack this positive status. After all, these beliefs are the outputs of a belief-independent process, which is straightforwardly unreliable. While Lyons embraces this consequence, those who feel the force of the New Evil Demon intuition may be left dissatisfied.

Second, we might question whether conditional reliability is, on its own, anything to write home about. Suppose Ken believes a host of absurdities: The moon is made of cheese, techno music is the highest form of art, cats are better than dogs, and so on. And suppose Ken infers the conjunction of these beliefs. In doing so, he uses a conditionally reliable belief-forming process. But does this mean that his resulting conjunctive belief has some valuable epistemic property, albeit one that falls shy of justification? This seems dubious. Intuitively, his conjunctive belief is just as absurd, and just as epistemically criticizable, as the most epistemically offensive of its conjuncts.

Blamelessness. An alternative answer is to say that while Renée's beliefs are not justified, they are epistemically *blameless* (Williamson forthcoming). Proponents of this approach emphasize that there is a distinction between (i) complying with a norm *N*, (ii) blamelessly violating *N*. For example, suppose the speed limit is 60 mph. Suppose my speedometer has just stopped working, but I have no reason to suspect it is broken. As a matter of fact, I am driving 61 mph, but my speedometer says I'm doing 59. I have broken the norm set by the speed limit, but I have done so blamelessly, because I have a good excuse for my violation.

I think proponents of this response are right that *norm violation* can come apart from *blameworthiness*. However, it's not clear that this gives us a full solution to the problem, for two reasons. First, there is a residual intuition that

---

[24] Why doesn't it rise to the level of justification? According to Goldman (1979) and Lyons (2013), an inferential belief that is the result of a conditionally reliable process is only justified if that process is operating on *justified* inputs.

Renée is, in some sense, complying with her epistemic obligations. Suppose Renée has the perceptual experience of sipping a coffee. What doxastic state should she adopt? Should she believe she is *not* sipping coffee? Should she suspend judgment on the question altogether? Neither seems right. This provides some reason to think that Renée is not merely blameless for holding her beliefs. She is – in some sense – believing as she should (cf. Schechter 2017).

There is also a more general worry about the bullet-biting response. Proponents of the bullet-biting response are committed to an error theory. They claim that when we intuit that Renée's belief is justified, we are making a mistake. Specifically, we are confusing two distinct statuses: Justification and blamelessness. (Other versions of the bullet-biting response will say something similar, just swapping out blamelessness with another epistemic status.) But it is questionable whether we have any independent reason to think that people are systematically confused on the distinction between justification and blamelessness.

These concerns provide some motivation for considering alternatives to the bullet-biting response. Is there any way to square reliabilism with the intuition that Renée's beliefs are justified?

3.1.3 Attributor Reliabilism

One strategy for reconciling reliabilism with the New Evil Demon intuition is to reconsider which worlds to use when evaluating the reliability of a process. A process can be reliable at one world, but unreliable at another. Perception is reliable at our world (we hope!), but not at Renée's world. The New Evil Demon objection tacitly assumes that reliability should be indexed to the world inhabited by the *subject* of the justification ascription (i.e., the believer's world). But perhaps we should reject this assumption.

If reliability is not indexed to the subject's world, then what world should we use when assessing processes for reliability? One possibility is to index it to the world of the *attributor* – that is, the person who is ascribing justification. Here's one way of fleshing this out:

> *Attributor Reliabilism:* An utterance of "A's belief is justified" is true, as evaluated at a world of evaluation w iff A's belief is formed by a process that is reliable at w (i.e., A's belief-forming process is disposed to produce true rather than false beliefs at w).[25]

---

[25] Indexing maneuvers are discussed by Sosa (1993) and Comesaña (2002). The latter defends a view on which justification ascriptions are ambiguous between two different readings, depending on whether reliability is indexed to the actual world or the world of the believer. For a closely related view, see Goldman's "two-stage" or "approved list" reliabilism (Goldman 1992; Fricker 2016).

How does this help with Renée and the Demon? The key idea is that the world of evaluation might differ from the world inhabited by the subject of the justification ascription. Suppose we ascribe justification to Renée by saying, for example:

(1) Renée is justified in believing there is a tree in front of her.

Let '@' denote *our world* – the world of people attributing justification to Renée by uttering (1). According to Attributor Reliabilism, we will evaluate the reliability of Renée's belief-forming process at @, not at the demon world (w_D) which Renée inhabits. Since perception is reliable at @, Attributor Reliabilism predicts that our utterance of (1) is true.

Is this solution satisfactory? Consider the demonic architect of Renée's world. Suppose this demon, sitting atop their demon throne in their demon world (w_D), is watching over Renée. This demon pronounces:

(2) Renée is not justified in believing there is a tree in front of her.

Attributor Reliabilism predicts that (2) is true, as evaluated at w_D.

We can take this argument a step further. Suppose this demon now turns his gaze toward @ and considers *us*, and pronounces:

(3) Their perceptual beliefs are not justified.

Attributor reliabilism predicts that (3) is also true, as evaluated at w_D.

Whether this is a devastating problem is open for debate. Attributor reliabilists may retort that we don't have clear pre-theoretic intuitions about the truth-values of justification ascriptions at distant worlds. Rather, when we evaluate a justification ascription for truth or falsity, we are evaluating it for truth or falsity at our world. Attributor Reliabilism predicts that (2) and (3) are false as evaluated at our world.

3.1.4 Normal Worlds Reliabilism

Another option is to index reliability to *normal worlds*:

> *Normal Worlds Reliabilism:* S's belief is justified iff it is formed by a process that is reliable in normal worlds.

The guiding thought is that Renée's demon world is *abnormal*. Perhaps the abnormality of her circumstances is what deprives her belief of justification. But how should we understand this notion of "normal worlds"?

Goldman's Account of Normal Worlds. In *Epistemology and Cognition*, Goldman suggested that the normal worlds are worlds consistent with our "general beliefs" about the sorts of objects, processes, and events that obtain in the world (1986: 107). This definition makes normality dependent on whatever we happen to believe about the world. Some have wondered whether this dependence makes the notion ill-suited to play a foundational role in a theory of justification. Pollock and Cruz (1999) raise the worry that if our general beliefs about the world are not themselves justified, then they shouldn't get to play a role in determining the justificatory status of beliefs. Graham (forthcoming) raises the concern that these general beliefs about the world may turn out to be inconsistent. If so, does that mean that there are no normal worlds? Yet another worry is that this way of defining normality reintroduces the sort of relativity that some find troubling about Attributor Reliabilism. Imagine a demon world where it is generally known that perception is unreliable. The worlds that are normal from the perspective of that world will be other demon worlds.

Faced with these objections, some might be tempted to abandon Normal Worlds Reliabilism altogether. But perhaps that would be too hasty. Perhaps we should instead cast about for a different understanding of normal worlds ...

Functionalist Accounts of Normal Worlds. Another option is to relativize normality to belief-forming processes:

Process-Relative Normal Worlds: The normal worlds, for a belief-forming process X, are those where conditions are normal for the operation of X.

On this account, different sets of worlds will be "normal" for different belief-forming processes.

This might just seem to push things back a step: How should we understand "conditions that are normal for the operation of a belief-forming process"? One strategy is to unpack this notion in functionalist terms. Roughly:

Functionalist Account of Normality: The conditions that are normal for the operation of a process X are conditions in which X can fulfill its function.

Versions of this idea have been developed, in somewhat different forms, by Burge (2003, 2010), Graham (2012, forthcoming), Kelp (2019), and Simion (2019).[26]

Applied to Renée: Renée has the misfortune of inhabiting a world where her perceptual systems cannot fulfill their functions. After all, the function of

---

[26] There are several differences between these accounts. For example, Burge develops his account in terms of status he calls "epistemic warrant," and is focused on giving a view of epistemic warrant for perceptual beliefs. On Simion's account, a belief is epistemically justified if it is generated by a properly functioning cognitive process, where a cognitive process is properly functioning just in case it produces knowledge. Thus Simion's account could be viewed as a version of the sort of "knowledge first" reliabilism mentioned in Section 1.

perceptual systems is to accurately track various features of the world. Renée's demonic deceiver has ensured that her perceptual systems cannot do this at her world (w_D). If she were in a world like ours, Renée's perceptual systems would be able to fulfill their functions. Consequently, the normal worlds for Renée's belief-forming process are worlds like ours.

How should we understand talk of the "function" of belief-forming processes? One influential approach explains functions in etiological terms. On Wright's (1973) account:

> *Wright Functions:* The function of X is Z iff:
>
> (1) X is there because it does Z, and
> (2) Z is a consequence of X's being there.

For example, the function of the heart is to pump blood because (i) hearts are around because they pump blood; and (ii) pumping blood is a consequence of hearts being there. Applied to a belief-forming process such as vision, one might hold that the function of vision in creatures like us is to enable accurate representation of distal objects in one's environment. This is because (i) creatures like us have vision because it enables such representations; and (ii) enabling accurate representations of distal objects is a consequence of vision.

This is an attractive approach. But I want to highlight a complication. The foregoing paragraph applied a Wright-style etiological account of function to vision in creatures like us. What about creatures like Renée? We are not told Renée's biographical or biological backstory. If Renée came from a world like ours and was transplanted to a demon world, the etiological account will say her vision has the same function that vision has at our world. But what if Renée and her ancestors always inhabited a demon world? What if Renée's vision (and that of her ancestors) never managed to accurately track features of the world? Then a Wright-style account of functions seems to predict that vision in Renée has no function, or, at least, it does not have the function of accurately tracking features of the world. So we seem to be saddled with the result that, in this version of the story, there are no normal worlds for Renée – no worlds, that is, where conditions are normal for the operation of her perceptual systems.

Some might embrace this result: If Renée really comes from a world where vision has no function at all, then her perceptual beliefs are not justified.[27] But some might find this a bitter pill to swallow. We might wonder: Is this really more palatable than the more straightforward bullet-biting response (Section 3.1.2)?

---

[27] See for example, Lyons (2013), Lasonen-Aarnio (forthcoming), and Graham (forthcoming).

Parallels in the Theory of Knowledge. Normal Worlds Reliabilism remains a topic of continued interest among epistemologists. It also parallels recent proposals in the theory of knowledge. Several philosophers in the last decade have proposed broadly reliabilist accounts of knowledge where normality plays a prominent role. For example, Greco (2014) offers an information-theoretic analysis of knowledge, indebted to Dretske (1981), according to which:

Information-Theoretic Analysis of Knowledge: A knows p iff both:

(1) A is in a state that carries the information that p, and
(2) A's being in this state causes or constitutes S's believing that p.

According to Greco, the notion of "carrying information" itself can be cashed out in terms of normality:

Normality Analysis of "Carrying Information": A is in a state s that carries the information that p iff both:

(1) Whenever conditions are normal, A is in s only if p, and
(2) Conditions are normal.

Another normality-based account of knowledge comes from Beddor and Pavese (2020), who defend a variant of a safety condition on knowledge (Section 1). Rather than defining safety in terms of nearby worlds, they define it in terms of normal worlds. Specifically:

Normality-Based Safety: Suppose an agent A believes p at w, using process X. A's belief that p amounts to knowledge iff p is true in all worlds w' where both:

(1) S believes p using X, and
(2) Conditions are at least as normal for the operation of X as those which obtain at w.[28]

Unlike Greco's version of Dretske's analysis, this theory allows that knowledge is possible even when conditions are abnormal. What's required is that your belief-forming process must get things right not just in your abnormal circumstances, but also in circumstances that are more normal than yours.

A full discussion of these views is outside the scope of this Element. The important point is that Normal Worlds Reliabilism is not without precedent or parallel. It bears an intriguing resemblance to various recent theories of knowledge.

Let's now switch gears and consider challenges to the idea that reliability is *sufficient* for justification.

---

[28] See also Goodman and Salow (2018) for a related account.

3.2 Clairvoyants & Rogue Neurosurgeons

3.2.1 The Challenge

According to Simple Process Reliabilism, reliability is sufficient for justification: If someone's belief is the result of a reliable process, then their belief is justified. The person does not need to know, or justifiably believe, or even have reason to believe that their belief was reliably formed.

This feature of reliabilism gives rise to a family of counterexamples. These counterexamples share the following structure: An agent forms a belief through a process that happens to be reliable, but the agent does not have any good reason to think they are using a reliable process. Consider:

> *Norman* (Bonjour 1980) Norman happens to be a clairvoyant. His clairvoyance is highly reliable: whenever he gets a compelling clairvoyant hunch about some matter, his hunch is invariably correct. However, Norman has never bothered to check the reliability of his clairvoyance; indeed, he has no evidence for or against the presence of this clairvoyant faculty. One day while eating breakfast Norman gets a clairvoyant hunch that the U.S. president is in New York. Based on his hunch, Norman comes to believe the president is in New York.

By stipulation, Norman's belief is the result of a reliable process. So, according to Simple Process Reliabilism, his belief is justified. But, according to BonJour, this is wrong: Norman's belief is *not* justified.

In support of this claim, BonJour considers two possibilities. The first is that Norman believes he has clairvoyance, and this belief is part of his basis for thinking the president is in NY. But, BonJour asks, "is it not obviously irrational, from an epistemic standpoint, for Norman to hold such a belief when he has no reasons at all for thinking that it is true or even for thinking that such a power is possible?" (1980: 62). If the answer is *yes* – as BonJour implies – then, BonJour contends, Norman's belief about the president's whereabouts is also irrational.

The second possibility is that Norman does not believe he has clairvoyance. In that case, BonJour claims, Norman's beliefs are deeply puzzling:

> From his standpoint, there is apparently no way in which he *could* know the President's whereabouts. Why then does he continue to maintain the belief that the President is in New York City? Isn't the mere fact that there is no way, as far as he knows or believes, for him to have obtained this information a sufficient reason for classifying this belief as an unfounded hunch and ceasing to accept it? And if Norman does not do this, isn't he thereby being epistemically irrational and irresponsible? (1980: 62–63)

Consequently, BonJour contends, Norman's belief about the president's whereabouts is "epistemically irrational and irresponsible, and thereby unjustified, whether or not he believes himself to have clairvoyant power" (1980: 63).

Structurally similar examples abound:

> *Truetemp.* (adapted from Lehrer 1990) Truetemp goes to the doctor for what he thinks will be routine brain surgery. Truetemp's doctor has other ideas; unbeknownst to Truetemp, she is an inventor and experimental neurosurgeon with little regard for informed consent or IRBs. While Truetemp is under anaesthesia, his doctor implants a device of her own devising, a "Tempucomp." One part of the Tempucomp is an extremely accurate thermometer affixed to Truetemp's scalp. Another part of the Tempucomp is a computational device in Truetemp's brain, capable of generating thoughts. The thermometer reliably transmits its readings of the ambient temperature to the computational component, which generates the corresponding thoughts in Truetemp's brain. The doctor does not tell Truetemp about any of this; when he wakes up, he has no idea that he has such a device implanted in his brain. After leaving the hospital, Truetemp finds himself struck by the thought that is exactly 74.5 degrees outside. He consequently believes that it is exactly 74.5 degrees outside, but never bothers to check this against any other source of information.

Truetemp's belief is produced by a reliable process (the Tempucomp). So if reliability were sufficient for justification, his belief would be justified. But, Lehrer claims, this is intuitively incorrect. To see the pull of this intuition, note that his belief about the temperature is extremely specific: exactly 74.5 degrees. Most ordinary humans cannot tell the temperature with such precision. Since TrueTemp has no reason to think he has had a Tempucomp in his head, he has no reason to think that he is different from ordinary humans in this respect.

3.2.2 Attributor Reliabilism and Normal Worlds Reliabilism, Reprised

Can the problem be avoided? One natural thought is that we could redeploy some of the maneuvers developed in response to the New Evil Demon Problem. Take Attributor Reliabilism. Applied to Norman: Attributor reliabilists might argue that clairvoyance is not reliable in the actual world. In our world, people who form beliefs about the locations of distant objects on the basis of hunches tend to be mistaken about them. So we can correctly judge:

(4) Norman's belief that the president in New York is unjustified.

This attribution is true relative to our world of evaluation (@).

It is, however, less straightforward to apply this maneuver to Truetemp. After all, the process responsible for Truetemp's belief about the temperature is something like: *forming beliefs about the temperature based on a Tempucomp* – call this process "*T*." Since *T* has never been instantiated in the actual world, it is unclear how to assess it for reliability.

Some might think there is an easy fix: just expand our domain of evaluation. Specifically, we could revise Attributor Reliabilism to say that an ascription of the form, "A's belief is justified" is true at a world of evaluation *w* iff A's belief was produced by a process that tends to produce true beliefs at the nearest worlds to *w* where that process is instantiated. Applied here, the idea would be that the ascription:

(5) Truetemp's belief about the temperature is justified.

is true at our world (@) iff *T* tends to produce true rather than false beliefs at the nearest worlds to @ where *T* is instantiated. But at the nearest worlds to @ where *T* is instantiated, it does tend to produce true beliefs. (After all, we stipulated that the Tempucomp functions extremely well, never yielding errors about the temperature.) So this approach would still predict Truetemp's belief is justified.

Similar points hold for Normal Worlds Reliabilism. Consider first Goldman's version of the view, where the normal worlds are those worlds consistent with many of our general beliefs about the world. As Goldman notes, there is a widespread belief that clairvoyance is not reliable, so at all normal worlds (in Goldman's sense) this process will be unreliable. In other worlds, *Norman ain't normal*! However, it is less clear that this helps with Truetemp, since ordinary people don't have beliefs about the reliability of Tempucomps.

What if we go the functionalist route, identifying the normal worlds for a process *X* with those worlds where conditions are conducive to the fulfillment of *X*'s function? Any such account should allow for functions that are derived from intentions. For example, the reason why the function of the gas gauge in my car is to indicate the fuel level is that it was *designed* to indicate the fuel level. Similarly, the Tempucomp was designed to accurately record the ambient temperature and to transmit these recordings to a person's brain. So the worlds where the Tempucomp fulfills this function will be worlds where the Tempucomp is reliable. Once again, we have failed to find an explanation that predicts that Temp's belief-forming process is unreliable.

3.2.3 Primal Systems

Another response to these counterexamples has been developed by Lyons (2009). A distinctive feature of BonJour and Lehrer's examples is that our characters' belief-forming processes have a somewhat unusual etiology. This is particularly clear in the case of Truetemp, whose heat-detecting abilities result from a newfangled technology surreptitiously implanted into his brain. Things are less clear-cut in the case of Norman; BonJour does not tell us where Norman's clairvoyance comes from. But, according to Lyons, the example suggests that Norman's clairvoyance stems from some recent development, such as "a recent encounter with radioactive waste" or a "neurosurgical prank" (2009: 118–119).

This leads Lyons to suggest both a diagnosis of the source of the problem and a proposed fix. The diagnosis: The etiology of Norman and Truetemp's beliefs deprives their beliefs of justification. Specifically, their beliefs are not justified because they are not produced by what Lyons call a "primal system," where a primal system is roughly akin to a module (in the sense of Fodor 1983). An important feature of primal systems, as Lyons understands them, is that they involve some combination of learning and innate constraints. This characteristic is not shared by either Truetemp's Tempucomp or Norman's clairvoyance. For example, the surgically implanted Tempucomp is neither innate nor the result of learning.

This diagnosis also suggests a solution. According to Lyons, in order for a non-inferential belief to be justified, it's not enough for it to be reliably formed. It must also be the result of a primal system.

Lyons supports this solution by offering variants of Norman, for example:

> *Nyrmoon* (adapted, with slight modifications, from Lyons 2009). Nyrmoon belongs to an extraterrestrial species that have evolved a form of highly reliable clairvoyance. For them, clairvoyance functions as a normal perceptual faculty. (It works by picking up highly attenuated energy signals from distant events, which members of their species experience as strong "hunches.") However, Nyrmoon is so unreflective that he has never bothered to form any beliefs about the reliability of his clairvoyance. One day, while eating his breakfast he gets a clairvoyant hunch that his president is currently in Nu Yark (a large city on their planet). Based on this hunch, he comes to believe his president is currently in NY Yark.[29]

Lyons claims that Nyrmoon's belief is intuitively justified, unlike Norman's. What explains this difference? The answer, says Lyons, lies in the etiology of their belief-forming processes. Nyrmoon's belief is the result of a primal system; it is part of his innate cognitive endowment.

While this is an ingenious solution, two points are worth noting. First, the primal systems view is not the only possible explanation for why Nyrmoon's belief is justified. Another relevant feature of the case is that clairvoyance is an

---

[29] Lyons also offers a structurally similar example of an extraterrestrial, Vipertemp, with a primal system that functions to detect ambient heat – a case designed to resemble Truetemp.

evolved trait in Nyrmoon's species, and has acquired the function of tracking distant events through this evolutionary process. Thus, the functionalist version of Normal Worlds Reliabilism will agree that Nyrmoon's belief is justified.[30]

Second, we might question this shared assumption that the etiology of a belief-forming process plays such a crucial role in determining justificatory status. Consider the following variant:

> *Noramoon.* Nyrmoon has a cousin, Noramoon, who was born with a birth defect depriving her of the clairvoyant abilities of her conspecifics. But an hour after her birth she was exposed to some radioactive waste. By a stroke of luck (the sort of luck that is the bread and butter of superhero origin stories), this causes her to develop a clairvoyant ability that is even more reliable than that of her fellow clairvoyants. She likewise forms the belief that the president is in NuYark.

Lyons' proposal predicts that whereas Nyrmoon's belief is justified, Noramoon's belief is not. Is this prediction correct? Different readers may have different intuitions here, and it is not my goal to try to legislate which intuitions are correct. But, speaking for myself, I am inclined to think that Noramoon's belief is just as justified as Nyrmoon's.

Now, there is an interesting question as to *why* Noramoon's belief is justified (assuming it is), whereas Norman's belief is not. One possible answer is that Noramoon belongs to a species whose members have evolved clairvoyant powers, unlike Norman. If so, then perhaps the etiology of the belief-forming process is still relevant to justification, just in a more indirect way: Perhaps we need to look at the etiology of sufficiently similar belief-forming processes characteristic of that agent's species. Another possible answer is to appeal to subtle differences in Noramoon's background information and Norman's background information. I explore this alternative answer in Section 3.2.5.

3.2.4 Agent Reliabilism

Another variant of reliabilism has been defended by John Greco under the banner of "agent reliabilism" (1999, 2000, 2003). Agent reliabilism claims that in order for a belief to be justified, it's not enough for it to be produced by a reliable belief-forming process. Rather, the belief must result "from stable and reliable dispositions that make up [the agent's] cognitive character." (J. Greco 1999: 287–288) And this in turn requires that the dispositions are both stable and "well integrated with [the agent's] other cognitive dispositions." (J. Greco 2003: 74)

---

[30] See Graham (2011), Goldman (2011b), and Ghijsen (2016) for versions of this point.

Could agent reliabilism solve our problems? It might seem the answer is *yes*. Agent reliabilists might argue that Norman's clairvoyance is not well integrated with his other cognitive dispositions, in which case his clairvoyant belief would not be justified. (Likewise with Truetemp and his Tempucomp.)

But how should we understand this notion of cognitive integration? Greco offers some remarks on the matter: "one aspect of cognitive integration concerns the range of outputs – if the products of a disposition are few and far between, and if they have little relation to other beliefs in the system, then the disposition is less well integrated on that account." (2003: 74) But, as Greco acknowledges, we can imagine a version of the Norman scenario where this condition is met. Perhaps every day Norman finds himself forming a belief about the distant location of some object or person. And suppose all of the resultant beliefs are logically consistent with the beliefs he forms through his other senses. So they are coherent with these other beliefs, in at least this minimal sense.[31,32]

In other passages, Greco suggests that in order for a disposition to be well integrated with an agent's cognitive character, it must be responsive to "dispositions governing counterevidence that disallow his clairvoyant belief." (2003: 475) The suggestion here seems to be that Norman has counterevidence which defeats his belief. This is an intriguing suggestion, and I think it is onto something important. But it deserves further scrutiny. Does Norman have defeating counterevidence? Let's take a closer look ...

3.2.5 Appealing to Defeat

The idea that Norman has defeating counterevidence has been defended independently, by philosophers who do not subscribe to agent reliabilism. Here, for example, is Goldman (1986):

> BonJour describes this case as one in which Norman possesses no evidence or reasons of any kind for or against the general possibility of clairvoyance, or for or against the thesis that he possesses it. But it is hard to envisage this description holding. Norman ought to reason along the following lines: 'If

---

[31] Similar points apply to Truetemp. Now, Truetemp forms his beliefs about the temperature as the result of a surgically implanted device. But presumably this is no barrier to justification. Suppose someone unwittingly undergoes cataract surgery (a common procedure through which a naturally cloudy lens is surgically replaced with an artificial lens). If their visual acuity is improved, couldn't they be justified in their resulting visual beliefs? Agent reliabilists can grant this point: they will presumably say that the vision of someone who has unknowingly undergone cataract surgery is sufficiently integrated with their other cognitive dispositions to render their beliefs justified. But then why not say the same about Truetemp?

[32] See also Cohen (2003) and Bernecker (2008) for arguments that agent reliabilism struggles to handle clairvoyance cases.

I had a clairvoyant power, I would surely find some evidence for this. I would find myself believing things in otherwise inexplicable ways, and when these things were checked by other reliable processes, they would usually check out positively. Since I lack any such signs, I apparently do not possess reliable clairvoyant processes.' (Goldman 1986: 112)

Call this the "defeater diagnosis." There is, I think, something very attractive about this proposal. Norman's absence of any evidence in favor of his clairvoyance is itself evidence that he lacks clairvoyance. Moreover, Norman presumably lacks evidence that anyone else has reliable clairvoyant powers. (If he's like us, he is even aware of self-proclaimed clairvoyants who turned out to be cranks.) Here too, this absence of evidence is itself evidence – specifically, evidence that people do not possess clairvoyant abilities. Arguably, these features of his background information are partially responsible for the intuition that Norman's belief is not justified.

A similar diagnosis extends to Truetemp: He has all sorts of indirect evidence that he does not have a Tempucomp in his head (what are the odds?), and that consequently he is an ordinary human, who is incapable of detecting the temperature with such fine-grained precision. And this evidence seems like it is part of what diminishes the justificatory status of his belief.

One way of testing the defeater diagnosis is to consider a variant of Norman where he has not yet acquired any defeating evidence. I present to you:

Baby Norman. Baby Norman has highly reliable clairvoyance. Being a baby, has never had the opportunity to check the reliability of his clairvoyance, or to amass any track record evidence of its reliability. As he lies in his crib, he forms all sorts of beliefs using his senses. He uses his vision to form the belief that his mother is standing over his crib. He uses his hearing to form the belief that the dog is barking. And he uses his clairvoyance to form the belief that his father is in the kitchen.

In this version of the case, the line of reasoning that Goldman suggests Norman should engage in – *If I had a clairvoyant power, I would surely have found some evidence for this by now. Since I have found no evidence for this, this is evidence that I lack a clairvoyant power* – is inapplicable. Is baby Norman's clairvoyant belief that his father is in the kitchen justified?

Speaking for myself, I am inclined to think the answer is *yes*. At the very least, it seems that there is an important justificatory difference between adult Norman's belief and his infant counterpart's. To draw out this intuition, recall BonJour's contention that it would be *irrational* for (adult) Norman to think the president is in NY, since it is irrational for him to think he has clairvoyance. By contrast, it does not seem that it is irrational for baby Norman to hold his clairvoyant belief concerning his father's whereabouts. For those who share the judgment that there is an important justificatory difference between our two Normans, this suggests that the defeater diagnosis is on the right track.

Let me briefly consider two ways of pushing back against the defeater diagnosis. First, even those who agree that there is a justificatory difference between baby Norman and adult Norman may still have the residual intuition that there is something epistemically amiss about baby Norman's clairvoyant belief. Specifically, some might think that his clairvoyant belief is less justified than, say, his visual or auditory beliefs. (See Graham 2017.) I confess that I do not share this residual intuition myself. But my goal here is not to dictate what people's intuitions should be. Rather, I will just note that there is nothing to prevent us from combining the defeater diagnosis with one of the other responses to the clairvoyance objection discussed in this section, such as Normal Worlds Reliabilism or the primal systems view. According to this "combination response," baby Norman's clairvoyant belief is less than fully justified, because of its strange etiology. But adult Norman's clairvoyant belief is in even worse epistemic shape, since it is held in the face of defeating evidence.

Second, some might wonder how the defeater diagnosis applies to Lyons' Nyrmoon variant, described earlier. The point of the Nyrmoon case was to describe an agent who is doxastically and phenomenally indistinguishable from Norman, but where the belief-forming process differs in its etiology. But if Norman and Nyrmoon are doxastically and phenomenally indistinguishable, it seems that they should be on a par with respect to whether their beliefs are defeated: If Norman's belief is defeated, the same should be true of Nyrmoon's.

However, as Ghijsen (2016: 95) observes, the description of the Nyrmoon case makes it natural to assume that Nyrmoon has used his clairvoyant system before and has accumulated some track record evidence about its reliability, even if he has not explicitly reflected on this track record. Moreover, since Nyrmoon is from a species of aliens that all share this clairvoyant ability, it's natural to assume that Nyrmoon has at least some evidence that other members of his species have reliable clairvoyance. Similar remarks apply to Noramoon. In this regard, Nyrmoon and Noramoon's situation differs from Norman's. Of course, we can modify the case to block these assumptions: We can stipulate that Nyrmoon has never received any evidence that he has reliable clairvoyance, and he has no reason to suspect that any members of his species have this faculty either. (Perhaps he even has misleading evidence that any other members of his species who claim to have clairvoyance are frauds.) But once we make these stipulations explicit, it is much less obvious that Nyrmoon's belief is justified. In this version of the case, we might well expect him to reason along the lines suggested by Goldman (*if I had clairvoyance, wouldn't I have seen some evidence of this by now?*).

So the defeater diagnosis enjoys some plausibility. But even if it gets the cases right, it faces an obvious challenge. The notions of defeat and evidence are clearly epistemic. How can we explicate these notions in non-epistemic terms? As we are about to see, the phenomenon of defeat poses a problem for reliabilists independently of Norman and Truetemp.

3.3 Defeat

3.3.1 Why Reliabilists Have a Problem with Defeat

This brings us to another problem for reliabilism: handling defeat. Consider a stock example:

> *Seeing Red* Dina is visiting an art exhibit. She comes across a sculpture which appears to be red; consequently, she believes: *The sculpture is red* ('RED'). A moment after she forms this belief a member of the museum staff, Steph, tells Dina that it is actually a white sculpture; the artist has illuminated it with cleverly disguised red lights.

Intuitively, Dina was justified in believing RED before talking with Steph. But Steph's testimony defeats this justification: After their conversation, Dina is no longer justified in believing RED.

What does reliabilism say? Suppose that the sculpture really was painted red, and there are no red lights; Steph was mistaken. And suppose Dina's eyesight is perfectly good. Then Dina's belief in RED is the result of good vision, operating in normal lighting conditions. This is a paradigmatic example of a reliable process. So reliabilism seems to wrongly predict that Dina is *still* justified in holding this belief, even after receiving Steph's testimony.

3.3.2 Process-Switching

There are various ways one might try to deal with this concern. One option is to hold that Steph's testimony changes the process responsible for Dina's belief. Before talking with Steph, Dina's belief in RED was the result of *vision*. But after their conversation, her belief acquires a more complex basis. Now, the relevant process is *vision while ignoring testimony that her vision was misleading in these circumstances*, or something to that effect. And this complex process is unreliable.[33]

In order for the process-switching defense to work in full generality, one would need to maintain that in every case where the agent who uses an otherwise reliable process gains a defeater, the acquisition of the defeater

---

[33] See Loughrist (2021) for a version of this approach. See Nagel (2021) for related ideas.

changes the process responsible for the agent's belief. But is there any principled reason for thinking this is true? Answering this question involves wading into the Generality Problem, to be discussed later in this section. But to preview: Many of the leading solutions to the Generality Problem give little hope of an affirmative answer. For example, one solution to the Generality Problem comes from the common-sense typing approach, according to which we should type belief-forming processes in accordance with the classificatory schemes that ordinary people are disposed to use in everyday conversation. Plausibly, these common-sense classifications will be fairly coarse-grained; ordinary people will be more likely to describe Dina's belief as the result of *vision*, rather than *using vision while ignoring testimony that her vision was likely to be misleading*. Or take causal approaches to the Generality Problem, according to which only factors that causally influence a belief should be mentioned when typing the belief-forming process. If absences are not causes, then Dina's failure to heed Steph's testimony is not a cause of Dina's post-testimony belief.

Even if we were to grant (*pace* the foregoing) that the acquisition of a defeater always changes the process type, this "process-switching" response faces a further question. Why think this new process will always be unreliable?[34] To stick with our example: Is there a principled reason to think that the process *using vision while ignoring testimony that her vision was misleading in these circumstances* is unreliable? A tempting answer is to say: While this complex process leads her to truth in Seeing Red, in many other circumstances it would lead her astray – just consider any situation where Dina's testimony is correct. And this fact counts against the reliability of the belief-forming process. There is, I think, something importantly right about this. But it remains an open question whether this point generalizes to all cases of defeat. I revisit this issue in Section 5.3, where I consider some arguments that someone who ignores relevant evidence is always going to form their beliefs in less reliable ways than someone who takes that evidence into account.

3.3.3 The Alternative Reliable Process Account (ARP)

To date, most reliabilists have responded to the problem of defeat by modifying the details of reliabilism. In Goldman's original 1979 statement and defense of reliabilism, he anticipates the problem of defeat. In response, he converts reliabilism into a theory of prima facie justification – where a belief is prima facie justified as long as it would be justified unless a defeater obtained. On Goldman's view, a belief is ultima facie justified (i.e., justified full stop) provided it is both prima facie justified and no defeater obtains:

---

[34] See Lasonen-Aarnio (2010) for discussion of this issue.

No Defeaters Process Reliabilism: An agent A's belief that p is (ultima facie) justified iff both:

(i) A's belief that *p* is the result of a reliable belief-forming process **(Prima facie justification clause)**, and
(ii) A's belief that *p* isn't defeated **(No defeaters clause)**.

But now we confront head-on the problem we raised in Section 3.2.5: Can we explain defeat in naturalistically respectable and, more particularly, reliabilist-friendly, terms?

Goldman (1979) suggested the answer is *yes*. He proposed to explain defeat in terms of the availability of certain alternative reliable processes (ARPs) that one could have used. More precisely:

Alternative Reliable Process Account of Defeat (ARP): A's belief that *p* is defeated iff there is some alternative reliable or conditionally reliable process that A could have used in addition to the process actually used, which would have resulted in A not believing *p*.[35]

What counts as an 'available' process? Goldman does not offer a precise definition. However, one natural thought is that we could define availability in terms of *ability*: A process is available to an agent as long as the agent is able to use that process.[36]

As Goldman notes, we might want to exclude some available processes from the scope of ARP:

[I]t seems implausible to say all 'available' processes ought to be used, at least if we include such processes as gathering new evidence. Surely a belief can sometimes be justified even if additional evidence-gathering would yield a different doxastic attitude. What I think we should have in mind here are such additional process as calling previously acquired evidence to mind, assessing the implications of that evidence, etc. (1979: 102)

Putting this together: We might say that a process is available as long as the agent has the ability to use it. And, following Goldman, we should tacitly restrict ARP to only those available processes that one can employ using the agent's current states as input.

With these clarifications in place, let's consider how this applies to Seeing Red. According to ARP, receiving Steph's testimony does not necessarily

---

[35] See also Lyons (2009) for a defense of this view. For closely related proposals, see Grundmann (2009) and Bedke (2010). The points I will raise in discussion also extend to these variants.
[36] To some extent this pushes the question back a step: how should we understand abilities? However, by now there is a large philosophical literature on the nature of abilities. (See Maier 2022 for an overview.) Proponents of ARP could appeal to the accounts in the literature to further flesh out their account of availability.

change Dina's belief-forming process; even after Dina chats with Steph, the process responsible for her belief in RED is *vision*. But Steph's testimony makes another process available to Dina: *believing Steph's testimony*. This is a reliable process (assuming Steph is generally reliable). And if Dina had used this process in addition to vision, she would have ceased believing RED. So ARP predicts that her belief is defeated.

While ARP delivers a promising treatment of many cases of defeat, it faces its own share of problems:

Defeater Defeat. One problem, raised briefly by Lyons (2009: 124) and developed in Beddor (2021), is that ARP is ill-equipped to handle cases where defeaters are themselves defeated. Here's one way of spelling out this worry (Beddor 2021):

> *Double Testimony.* As before, Dina sees what appears to be a red sculpture; consequently she believes RED (the sculpture is red). As before, Steph tells her that it is a white sculpture illuminated by cleverly disguised red lights. Immediately after Steph says this, the exhibit curator, Cora, swoops in and tells Dina that Steph is mistaking this exhibit for another one.

Intuitively, Cora's testimony defeats the defeater provided by Steph's testimony: After getting Cora's testimony, Dina regains some of her previous justification for believing RED. But what does ARP say about this case? Well, the process, *believing Steph's testimony* remains reliable (assuming Steph is generally reliable). And it remains available to Dina. So a straightforward application of ARP incorrectly predicts that Dina's belief in RED remains defeated.

Conditional Fallacy. Another concern for ARP comes from the fact that one might have a reliable process available without having a good reason to use that process. Here's an example from Beddor (2015a):

> *Thinking About Unger* Harry sees a tree in front of him; he consequently believes TREE: *There is a tree in front of me.* Now, Harry happens to be very good at forming beliefs about what Peter Unger's skeptical 1975 time-slice would advise him to believe in any situation. Call this process his 'Unger Predictor': in any situation, Harry's Unger Predictor spits out an accurate belief about what doxastic attitudes Unger's 1975 time-slice would advise an agent to adopt in that situation. Moreover, Harry has a high opinion of Unger's 1975 time-slice. Were he to realize that Unger would advise him to suspend judgment on some proposition, this would lead him to suspend judgment on that claim. So if Harry had used his Unger Predictor, he would have come to believe SUSPEND: *Unger would advise me (Harry) to suspend judgment regarding TREE.* This would, in turn, have caused Harry to suspend judgment regarding TREE.

Is Harry justified in believing TREE? Intuitively, *yes*. After all, he is seeing a tree in good lighting conditions. He has no reason to suspect conditions are abnormal, or that the light is playing a trick on him. But this intuition conflicts with ARP. His Unger Predictor is a reliable process. And if he were to use it, it would cause him to cease believing TREE.

A more general message can be gleaned from this example. It is one thing to have a reliable process that meets the counterfactual condition specified by ARP. It is another thing to have a good reason to use this process. Cases like Thinking About Unger suggest that the mere availability of such a process – in the absence of a good reason to use it – does not suffice for defeat (Beddor 2021; Graham and Lyons 2021).

We could revise ARP to accommodate this point:

> *Normative ARP:* A's belief that *p* is defeated iff there is some alternative reliable or conditionally reliable process that A could *and should* have used in addition to the process actually used, which would have resulted in A not believing *p*.

However, the "should" here is presumably not moral or prudential but *epistemic*. So, absent some further account of when one (epistemically) should use an alternative process, this normative variant tacitly abandons reliabilism's reductive aspirations.[37]

Taking stock: ARP faces serious problems.[38] Can these problems be overcome? If not, is a more promising reliabilist-friendly account of defeat forthcoming? We'll revisit these questions in the ensuing sections.

3.4 The Generality Problem

3.4.1 Typing Trouble

Process reliabilists say that a belief is justified if it is produced by a reliable process. But how should we individuate belief-forming processes? This question has been forcefully pressed by Conee and Feldman (1998), who contend that reliabilists lack a satisfactory answer.

---

[37] For discussion of some of other attempts to modify ARP to avoid this counterexample, and a discussion of further problems that await, see Beddor (2015a).

[38] Further problems are also in store. Beddor (2015a) also offers a counterexample to the necessity direction of ARP. Suppose Clarence is told by Masha that the department will be hiring next year. But then Victor subsequently tells Clarence that the search was canceled. Both Masha and Victor are generally reliable. But Clarence harbors a deep-seated hatred of Victor that causes him to disbelieve everything Victor says. Moreover, no amount of reflection would rid Clarence of this distrust. If Clarence has no good reason for this distrust, his belief that the department will be hiring is still defeated by Victor's testimony. But it's not clear that ARP delivers this result. Given his deep-seated distrust of Victor, is there any process *available* to Clarence which would cause him to believe Victor's testimony? See also Fumerton (1988) for further concerns about ARP.

Consider the following example adapted from Conee and Feldman (1998):

> *Smith's Vision* Smith looks out her window one sunny Tuesday afternoon and spots a maple tree. She forms the belief, *There is a maple tree near my house* ('MAPLE').

What is the process responsible for Smith's belief? Here are some candidates:

P1: Perception

P2: Vision

P3: Vision in good lighting conditions

P4: Believing there is a maple tree based on the visual experience of a maple tree

P5: Believing there is a maple tree based on the visual experience of a maple tree viewed from such-and-such a distance, in such-and-such lighting conditions

P6: Vision on a Tuesday afternoon

P7: Forming a belief about a maple tree on the basis of vision while wearing clean Converse shoes

The list can be continued indefinitely.

Now for the problem: All of these ways of describing the belief-forming process seem, in some sense, correct. That is, Smith's belief seems to be the result of perception **and** vision **and** vision in good lighting conditions, and so on. Any attempt to pick out a single "right" process seems arbitrary. To put the problem in more general terms: reliability attaches to process types. Any belief token is the result of many distinct process types.

3.4.2 Common-Sense Typing

One response to the Generality Problem – suggested as far back as Goldman's 1979 paper – is to turn to common sense for help. To illustrate the basic idea, try rereading Smith's Vision and ask yourself, "How would I describe the process responsible for Smith's belief in MAPLE?" You would find some answers more natural than others. For example, P2 (*vision*) and P3 (*vision operating in good lighting conditions*) seem like pretty natural answers. By contrast, few would be tempted to reply with P7 (*forming a belief about a maple tree on the basis of vision while wearing clean Converse shoes*). This suggests a simple approach to the Generality Problem:

> *Common-Sense Typing Approach*: The process type relevant to determining the justificatory status of a belief token most closely corresponds to our common sense classifications of belief-forming processes.

Conee and Feldman (1998) raise an important concern about this solution. According to them, P1–P5 are all common-sense classifications of Smith's belief-forming process, but they still differ in their reliability. So even if common sense enables us to reject, for example, P7 as an appropriate process type, it will not have winnowed down the range of eligible candidates to a single process type, or even a class of process types that do not differ substantially in their degrees of reliability.

Recent developments of the common-sense typing approach have sought to answer this objection. Both Jönsson (2013) and Olsson (2016) appeal to a body of work in psychology known as "basic-levels theory," pioneered by Eleanor Rosch (e.g., Rosch et al. 1976). Rosch and her colleagues showed participants pictures of an entity that fell into different categories formulated at different levels of generality – for example, something that could be classified as a Labrador, a dog, or an animal. Participants were then asked, "What would you call this?" Rosch and her colleagues found a striking degree of convergence in the responses. Specifically, intermediate level categories – "dog," in this example – were overwhelmingly preferred to more specific and more general categories. Building on this work, Olsson and Jönsson conjecture that people might similarly prefer intermediate level classifications for belief-forming processes. In the case of Smith's Vision, this intermediate level might be something P2 or P3, rather than a very general category (e.g., P1) or a very specific category (e.g., P5).

Jönsson (2013) reports empirical research supporting this conjecture. Jönsson recruited participants and showed them clips from the shows *CSI* and *CSI: Miami* in which a character arrives at some conclusion. Participants were asked how the character formed their belief (e.g., "How did Dominic come to believe there was a bomb in the school?"). Jönsson found a high degree of convergence in the verbs that participants used to describe the belief-forming process: For twelve of the sixteen prompts, over half of the participants converged on the same verb to describe the belief-forming process. In a follow-up experiment, Jönsson assigned participants to two conditions: In one condition, participants were asked to evaluate the level of reliability of the character's belief-forming process; in the other, participants were asked to evaluate the level of justification of the character's belief. Jönsson found a strong correlation between these judgments. This provides at least some evidence in support of the conjecture that there is a high level of convergence in common-sense process-typing classifications, and that these classifications are closely connected with assessments of justifiedness.

3.4.3 Cognitive Science for the Win?

Rather than turning to common-sense, we might look to cognitive science for guidance. Not every way of describing a belief-forming process carves psychological reality at its joints. Take P6 (*forming a belief about a maple tree on the basis of vision while wearing clean Converse shoes*). It's natural to think this is a belief-forming process in name only; it's not the sort of process we would expect to feature in a mature cognitive science.

But will cognitive science always single out a unique belief-forming process type responsible for a given belief? Conee and Feldman (1998) register doubts. Even if P6 is off the table, one might think that P1–P4 are all process descriptions that will have some role to play in cognitive science, in which case we will not have fully solved the problem.

Recently, there have been some sophisticated attempts to address this concern. Here I'll focus on Lyons' (2019) account, which is arguably the most fully developed version of this approach.

Lyons observes that cognitive science is replete with discussion of cognitive processes. For example, it is widely thought that dead reckoning is a different process than navigating from landmarks (Collett and Graham 2004; Gallistel 2007), and that visual facial recognition is a different process from the recognition of other visual stimuli (Peterson and Rhodes 2003). This gives us reason to think that Conee and Feldman's bleak prognosis about the solvability of the Generality Problem may be unduly pessimistic.

How should we understand the sort of cognitive processes invoked in cognitive science? According to Lyons, these cognitive processes are best understood as *information-processing algorithms*. These algorithms are relativized to various parameters: psychological variables that systematically affect algorithmic processing. Lyons offers as examples of such variables the vividness of the perceptual experience, the way attention is allocated, and the number (and perhaps salience) of potential distractors. The underlying thought is that there is an epistemic difference between visual recognition of a face (for example), and visual recognition of a face while distracted and exhausted.

Putting the pieces together, we get:

> *Algorithm and Parameters Characterization* (Lyons 2009): The process type relevant to determining the justificatory status of a belief token is the complete algorithmic characterization of every psychological process token causally relevant to that belief, along with the associated parameter variables for all those processes.

How would this apply to Smith's Vision? As Lyons notes, this approach predicts that the relevant way of characterizing belief-forming processes will usually be very specific. Since processing visual stimuli involves a different algorithm than auditory stimuli, the relevant type won't be something as general as *perception* (P1) – it will need to reference the sort of sensory modality in question. Since lighting conditions are a parameter that systemically affects visual processing, this will go into the characterization of the belief-forming process as well; so P2, P4, P6, and P7 will be ruled out as well. And since *allocation of attention* is another variable that systematically affects visual processing, it also won't be P3 (*vision in good lighting conditions*) or P5 (*believing there is a maple tree based on the visual experience of a maple tree viewed from such-and-such a distance, in such-and-such lighting conditions*). Rather, as Lyons notes, the process will rather be something of the form: *visual recognition for natural stimuli in lighting conditions L, with causally relevant retinal image size S, with attentional resources allocated in a manner M.*

3.4.4 Causal Approaches, Generally

Lyons' view can be seen as an instance of a more general family of approaches. The Algorithm and Parameters Characterization emphasizes factors that are *causally* relevant to the formation and maintenance of the token belief. It is thus a version of a "causal approach" to the Generality Problem, which seeks to solve the Generality Problem in terms of the factors that are causally relevant to the belief.

Other philosophers have also adopted causal approaches to the Generality Problem. For example, Becker (2008), building on Goldman (1986), proposes:

> *Narrowest Causally Operative Typing:* The process type relevant to determining the justificatory status of a belief token is the narrowest content-neutral belief-forming process that is causally operative in belief production.

The Algorithm and Parameters Characterization could be viewed as a special instance of the causal approach. It is the special instance that results from taking the narrowest content-neutral belief-forming process causally operative in belief production to always be characterizable in terms of every psychological process token causally relevant to that belief, along with the associated parameter variables for all those processes.

3.5 Taking Stock and Looking Ahead

This section reviewed some classic objections to reliabilist theories of justification, as well as some of the leading responses. Whether any of these responses is completely successful is the subject of ongoing debate. As we saw, some of these responses incur further difficulties or run afoul of variants of the cases they sought to solve.

Moreover, even if these responses on their own are individually successful, a further worry hovers in the background. The worry is this: We have not found a one-size-fits-all solution to reliabilism's woes. For example, one of the most promising solutions to the New Evil Demon problem, Normal Worlds Reliabilism, struggles to generalize to handle Truetemp; it also says nothing about defeat or the Generality Problem. So it seems that the best-case scenario is a piecemeal victory. Some might find this dissatisfying: Perhaps the absence of a unified solution is itself an indication of a deeper problem within reliabilism.

4 Evidence to the Rescue?

4.1 An Evidentialist Diagnosis and a Route Forward

In the previous section, we explored some problems for reliabilism. At this point, it is worth taking a step back and asking: Do the problems spring from a common source?

Here is a diagnosis some may find tempting: Reliabilism went astray because it left out a crucial ingredient in the recipe for justification: *evidence*. We've seen that reliabilism has historically been a rival to evidentialism. Unlike evidentialists, reliabilists do not forge any explicit connections between justification and evidence.[39] Perhaps this omission was the source of our reliabilist woes.

This diagnosis suggests a potential route forward. Perhaps we should modify our reliabilist framework to incorporate evidentialist elements.

This is a promising thought. No surprise, then, that over the past decade several philosophers have explored this strategy. While they differ in details, Comesaña (2006, 2010, 2018, 2020), Goldman (2011a), Tang (2015), and Miller (2018) all develop views that synthesize reliabilism with its erstwhile adversary, evidentialism.

But is the promise of a reliabilist-evidentialist reconciliation too good to be true? In this section, we'll see that developing a hybrid theory that cures all of our woes is easier said than done. Far from giving us the best of both worlds, it starts to look like a reliabilist-evidentialist hybrid may give us the worst of both, inheriting many of the problems facing both traditional reliabilism and evidentialism.

---

[39] Though one might argue that some notion of evidence was always *implicit* in traditional forms of reliablism, since reliable processes typically take certain states of the agent as inputs. More on this in the next section.

4.2 Evidential Basing, Clairvoyants, and Tempucomps

4.2.1 An Evidential Basing Requirement Introduced

What form should an evidential-reliabilist hybrid take? In an influential pair of papers, Comesaña (2006, 2010) recommends that reliabilists adopt an *evidential basing requirement*.

Comesaña starts by observing that any adequate epistemology needs to capture the distinction between two species of justification: *doxastic* and *propositional*. To illustrate the difference, suppose Hercule Poirot is investigating who murdered the duchess. All clues – the witness's testimony, the motives, the various alibis – indicate the groundskeeper did it. Moreover, Poirot believes the groundskeeper is guilty. But, in an uncharacteristic lapse of rationality, Poirot does not arrive at his belief by considering the evidence, but rather by consulting his ouija board (a new vogue at the time). Is he justified in his belief? Yes and no. On the one hand, all his evidence speaks in favor of believing the groundskeeper committed the crime. On the other hand, there is an important sense in which his doxastic state is defective, given the epistemically irresponsible fashion in which it is formed. In the lingo of epistemologists, he has *propositional justification* for holding this belief. But he lacks *doxastic justification*: His token belief state, as it is currently formed and maintained, is not justified.

Reliabilism is primarily a theory of doxastic justification: It says that a token belief is doxastically justified if and only if that token belief state is formed in a reliable manner.[40] Evidentialism is primarily a theory of propositional justification: It says that an agent is propositionally justified in believing *p* if and only if the agent's evidence supports believing *p*. However, evidentialists have a standard story to tell about doxastic justification. The key idea is to supplement evidentialism with a requirement that the agent's belief needs to be *based* on their evidence (e.g., Conee and Feldman 2004). This, according to evidentialists, is why Poirot's belief that the groundskeeper is not doxastically justified.

Comesaña suggests that reliabilists take this idea on board. To introduce the idea in its most minimal form, the suggestion is that we should impose the following necessary condition on justification:

> *Evidential Basing Requirement:* A's belief is justified only if it is formed by a reliable process that is based on some evidence possessed by A.

---

[40] As Goldman (1979) and Lyons (2009) note, there is a straightforward way of extending it to encompass propositional justification: agent *A* is propositionally justified in believing *p* iff there is some reliable process available to *A* which is such that, if *A* applied that process to *A*'s total cognitive state, it would result in a doxastically justified belief that *p*.

The Evidential Basing Requirement agrees with traditional reliabilism that reliability is a necessary condition on justification. But it denies that this is a sufficient condition. In this regard, Comesaña's proposal is not idiosyncratic. Virtually all extant reliabilist-evidentialist hybrids endorse some version of the idea that justification requires *both* reliability and (some form of) evidential support.

This feature of the view has an important consequence, which it is worth flagging. Any hybrid view that takes justification to be a matter of both reliability and evidential support has little hope of solving the New Evil Demon Problem. After all, the New Evil Demon Problem attacks the idea that reliability is *necessary* for justification. Comesaña (2010) acknowledges this point, but expresses optimism that the New Evil Demon Problem can be handled by other means.[41] To his credit, we have seen that there are some potentially promising solutions to the New Evil Demon Problem available. But it does mean that incorporating evidentialist elements into the theory is not a panacea: It does not solve all our problems at one fortuitous swoop.

What problems does the Evidential Basing Requirement solve? According to Comesaña, it solves the problem of Norman the clairvoyant and the Generality Problem. For ease of exposition, I will defer discussion of the Generality Problem until later in this section, focusing for now on the clairvoyance problem. Comesaña's solution is straightforward:

> Notice that one crucial feature of BonJour's example is that Norman has no evidence for or against his clairvoyant powers, or regarding the whereabouts of the President – the belief just "pops up" in his head. This is at least one of the reasons why we have the intuition that Norman is not justified in believing that the President is in New York City: because he doesn't base that belief on any evidence. (Comesaña 2010: 582)

One could provide a similar diagnosis of Truetemp: He does not have any evidence that it is exactly 74.5 degrees, or that he has some capacity that would enable him to accurately detect the temperature with such a degree of precision.

On the face of it, this is a neat solution. But does it work?

4.2.2 What is Evidence Possession, Again?

An important question for any reliabilist-evidentialist hybrid is whether it still retains the features that rendered reliabilism attractive in the first place. One of reliabilism's major selling points is its reductive potential: It promises to explain justification without recourse to any unreduced epistemic notions.

---

[41] Comesaña's preferred solution is a version of Attributor Reliabilism (Section 3.2).

But note that the Evidential Basing Requirement introduces an unreduced epistemic notion: *possessed evidence*. So we inherit one of the questions facing evidentialists (Section 2.3): What does it take to possess something as evidence?

In his 2010 paper, Comesaña takes a page from traditional evidentialist theories, proposing that someone's possessed evidence consists in some subset of their mental states. This is the start of an answer, but only a start. Which mental states, exactly? Some might be inclined to answer: Those which are accessible to the agent. But now we find ourselves in familiar waters (Section 2.3). Can we explain the relevant notion of accessibility in non-epistemic terms?

This is not to say that no suitable account of evidence possession can be provided. The next section explores whether we can make progress using reliabilist resources. The point is simply that going in for an Evidential Basing Requirement incurs some of the explanatory burdens facing evidentialists – burdens that Simple Process Reliabilism avoids.

4.2.3 Clairvoyants with Evidence?

Comesaña's solution hinges on the claim that Norman lacks any evidence bearing on the president's whereabouts. And this is how BonJour describes the case. But why doesn't Norman's clairvoyance count as a form of evidence? Imagine Norman's clairvoyant beliefs come to him as "hunches," which carry their own distinctive phenomenology. Maybe every time he has a clairvoyant hunch, a corresponding visual image pops into his mind, or he has a distinctive taste in his mouth, or a particular ringing in his ears. So when Norman exercises his clairvoyance to form the belief that the President is in New York, he is in some mental state CLAIR(*Pres, NY*). Why doesn't this mental state count as evidence? If it does, then the Evidential Basing Requirement is satisfied after all. (Similar points can be made using Truetemp.)

Some might try to argue that even if this mental state could qualify as evidence that Norman possesses, it isn't evidence *in favor of* the proposition that the President is in NY. In other words, we should unpack the Evidential Basing Requirement as follows:

> *Evidential Basing Requirement (Expanded):* A's belief p is justified only if
>
> (1) It is formed by a reliable process that takes as input some evidence e possessed by A, and
> (2) e supports believing p.

But we now run into a second question facing evidentialists (Section 2.3):

> *Evidential Support Question:* How should we understand evidential support? What does it take for *e* to support believing *p*?

For hybrid theorists, it's natural to try to explain evidential support using reliabilist resources, for example:

> *Reliabilist Support:* Evidence *e* supports believing *p* iff *e* reliably indicates *p*, i.e., the objective probability of *p*, given *e*, is sufficiently high.

However, this view gets our Norman variant wrong. Norman's mental state CLAIR(*Pres*, *NY*) reliably indicates the president is in NY. Suppose that only someone with reliable clairvoyance would have that particular mental state, with that particular phenomenology. Consequently, the objective probability that the U.S. President is in NY, given that Norman is experiencing CLAIR (*Pres*, *NY*) could be extremely high – indeed, it could be 1.

Perhaps this is just a symptom of a more general problem with Reliabilist Support. In his earlier work, Comesaña defended a reliabilist account of the evidential support relation.[42] But he subsequently revised his account, in view of examples like the following:

> *Unknown Symptoms* (adapted from Comesaña 2018: 316) A doctor in training is examining a patient who displays a certain pattern of symptoms *S*. Alas, our doctor in training has not studied the material, and he has no clue about what condition would cause symptoms *S*. Unbeknownst to him, *S* could only be caused by a particular condition *C*, and so the objective probability that the patient has *C*, given that they display symptoms *S*, is very high.

Given that the aspiring medic has no inkling of the connection between *S* and *C*, it seems wrong to say that *S* supports believing the patient has *C*.[43]

In light of examples like these, Comesaña now (2018, 2020) models evidential support using an evidential probability function, which is not itself explicable in terms of objective probabilities, or the ratio of true to false beliefs in some domain. But this in effect amounts to renouncing reliabilism's reductive ambitions.

---

[42] Or "fit," in Comesaña's terminology. Comesaña's (2010) view is very similar in spirit to Reliabilist Support, but includes extra complications to handle cases where the evidence itself contains various beliefs. See also Tang 2016 for a hybrid view that models support relations in terms of objective probabilities.

[43] Perhaps there is some purely objective sense of support in which *S* does support the hypothesis that the patient has *C*. But it doesn't seem *S* supports this hypothesis in the epistemic sense; it doesn't in any way contribute to our aspiring doctor's justification for believing the patient has *C*.

4.2.4 Too Restrictive?

Let me raise one more issue for the idea that we can handle Norman and TrueTemp using the Evidential Basing Requirement. The goal of introducing the Evidential Basing Requirement was to make our reliabilist account more restrictive, ensuring that certain beliefs that classic reliabilist theories endow with a stamp of epistemic approval get this approval rescinded. But in doing so, we should take care not to make our account overly restrictive.

Recall Lyons' example of Nyrmoon, who has evolved reliable clairvoyance. Lyons claims that Nyrmoon's clairvoyant beliefs are intuitively justified, unlike Norman's. It's unclear how the Evidential Basing Requirement could explain this difference. Even if we can give a principled reason for denying that Norman's belief is based on evidence – and so rule out the possibility that CLAIR(*Pres*, *NY*) counts as evidence – then, by parity of reasoning, it seems the same verdict should apply to Nyrmoon: His clairvoyant belief is not based on any evidence either. But then the Evidential Basing Requirement would not accommodate the intuition that there is a justificatory difference between their beliefs.

4.3 Evidence, Reliability, and Defeat

4.3.1 Defeat Revisited

As formulated, the Evidential Basing Requirement only says that the reliable process takes as input *some* evidence possessed by the agent. Consequently, it does not, taken on its own, explain why justification is absent in cases of defeat. Recall Seeing Red. There is a reliable process (vision) that takes Dina's visual experience of the red sculpture as input and produces a belief that the sculpture is red (RED) as output. Since this visual experience is part of her evidence, the Evidential Basing Requirement is satisfied.

A natural solution is to distinguish between partial and total evidence. While Dina has some evidence in favor of RED, her total evidence does not support believing this proposition. After all, her total evidence also includes Steph's testimony that it's a white sculpture illumined by red lights. And this more inclusive body of evidence does not, intuitively, support her belief. In other words, we should impose:

> *Total Evidence Requirement:* S's belief that *p* is justified only if S's *total* evidence supports believing *p*.

A version of a Total Evidence Requirement can be found in standard formulations of evidentialism.[44] A closely related idea is found in Bayesian epistemology, which requires agents to conditionalize on their total evidence. No surprise, then, that some version of a Total Evidence Requirement has been embraced by many reliabilist-evidentialist hybrids.[45]

In my eyes, the ability to handle cases of defeat is one of the strongest arguments in favor of the Total Evidence Requirement, and, by extension, of a reliabilist-evidentialist hybrid. That said, there is a question about where a Total Evidence Requirement should figure into our theory. Should we just tack it onto our theory of justification as an extra condition? That is, should we embrace a view on which justification involves two separate components, a reliability component and a Total Evidence Requirement?

Two Component View: A's belief p is justified iff both:

(i) It is produced by a reliable process (perhaps operating on certain evidence as input), and
(ii) A's total evidence supports believing p.[46]

I think this would be dissatisfying, for two reasons. The first is by now familiar. The Total Evidence Requirement relies on the notions of evidential possession and evidential support, which, given reliabilists' naturalistic aspirations, we would like to explain in non-epistemic terms. Second, there is a question as to *why* justification requires support by one's total evidence. Can we give any principled rationale for this requirement?

A natural thought is that evidential support is a reliable guide to the truth: beliefs that are supported by one's total evidence tend to be true. But if this thought is on the right track, then this suggests that a Total Evidence Requirement should not enjoy the status of a separate, *sui generis* condition on justification. Rather, the Total Evidence Requirement should itself be a consequence of a more general reliabilist account. (See Section 5 for discussion of what such an account might look like.)

---

[44] Recall Conee and Feldman's suggestion that an agent is only doxastically justified in believing p if there is no more inclusive body of evidence possessed by the agent that does not support believing p.
[45] While they differ in points of detail, Tang (2016) and Miller (2019) both impose some form of a Total Evidence Requirement. While a Total Evidence Requirement was not explicitly formulated in Comesaña (2010), his later formulations include a version of this idea (Comesaña 2018, 2020).
[46] Cf. Goldman (2011a), which defends a two component view of justification, though without going so far as to endorse the Total Evidence Requirement.

4.4 Evidence, Reliabilism, and the Generality Problem

4.4.1 Comesaña's Solution to the Generality Problem

So far, we have focused on whether incorporating evidence into a reliabilist framework helps with the objections to the idea that reliability is sufficient for justification. According to Comesaña (2006, 2010), appealing to evidence also solves the Generality Problem.

Recall that evidentialists explain doxastic justification in terms of the *basis* for the agent's belief. As we previously noted, Comesaña (2006, 2010) suggests that reliabilists should take a page from the evidentialist's playbook, and build evidential basing into their theory. Once they do, Comesaña thinks they will have a principled answer to the Generality Problem. More precisely, Comesaña defends:

> *Well-Founded Reliabilism:* For any token belief that *p*, which is based on evidence *e*, the relevant belief-forming process type will always be of the form: *forming a belief that p on the basis of evidence e.*

4.4.2 Revenge of the Generality Problem?

This is a clever solution; Comesaña proposes a way of converting the evidentialist's own account of justification into a solution to the Generality Problem. However, this response only works if the evidentialist's account of doxastic justification solves the Generality Problem. But closer inspection provides grounds for doubt on this score.

Take our earlier example used to illustrate the Generality Problem, Smith's Vision, where Smith looks out the window one sunny afternoon, sees a maple tree, and forms the belief, *There is a maple tree near my house* ('MAPLE') (Section 3.4.1). We saw that there are various ways of characterizing Smith's belief-forming process:

P1: Perception

P2: Vision

P3: Vision in good lighting conditions

P4: Believing there is a maple tree based on the visual experience of a maple tree

P5: Believing there is a maple tree based on the visual experience of a maple tree viewed from such-and-such a distance, in such-and-such lighting conditions

P6: Vision on a Tuesday afternoon

P7: Forming a belief about a maple tree on the basis of vision while wearing clean Converse shoes

According to Well-Founded Reliabilism, the relevant belief-forming process type is:

P8: Forming a belief in MAPLE on the basis of evidence e.

But how should we characterize the relevant evidence e? Here are some candidates:

E1: Perceptual experience

E2: Visual experience

E3: Visual experience in good lighting conditions

E4: Visual experience of a maple tree in good lighting conditions

E5: Visual experience of a maple tree viewed from such-and-such a distance, in such-and-such lighting conditions

E6: Visual experience on a Tuesday afternoon

E7: Visual experience of a maple tree while wearing clean Converse shoes

For each of these candidate bodies of evidence, there will be a corresponding process type:

P9: Forming in MAPLE on the basis of a perceptual experience.

P10: Forming a belief in MAPLE on the basis of a visual experience.

P11: Forming a belief in MAPLE on the basis of visual experience in good lighting conditions.

P12: Forming a belief in MAPLE on the basis of visual experience of a maple tree in good lighting conditions.

P13: Forming a belief in MAPLE on the basis of a visual experience of a maple tree from such-and-such a distance, in such-and-such lighting conditions.

P14: Forming a belief in MAPLE on the basis of a visual experience on a Tuesday afternoon.

P15: Forming a belief in MAPLE on the basis of a visual experience of a maple tree while wearing clean Converse shoes.

Some of these types are equivalent to some of our earlier types (P1–P7); others are close variants. Importantly, these types (P9–P15) may differ in their level of reliability. Which of these is the *right* type? Well-Founded Reliabilism does not tell us. The Generality Problem rears its head again.

In response, some might think we should identify *e* with a particular token experience:

E_{token}: The particular token experience Smith is undergoing at the moment of looking at the maple tree.

Thus the corresponding process type is:

P16: Forming a belief in MAPLE on the basis of E_{token}.

However, this solution runs into further difficulties. Suppose that E_{token} is a token visual experience of seeing a 5″ leaf with five lobes separated by deep margins. And suppose that only maple trees would produce this particular visual experience. Then the type, *forming a belief in MAPLE on the basis of E_{token}* is reliable. But suppose that Smith has no idea that maple trees have five lobes; moreover, these features of his experience play no causal role in the formation or maintenance of his belief. (Perhaps even if he saw a leaf with four lobes he would still believe it is a maple tree.) Then, intuitively, his belief is not justified.[47]

In short, Well-Founded Reliabilism faces a challenge when it comes to specifying the evidential basis for the agent's belief. This, in effect, amounts to a "new round" of the Generality Problem. One way of trying to avoid this new round would be to identify the relevant evidence with the particular token experience that the agent is undergoing. But this would lead to counterintuitive verdicts about whether an agent is justified in particular cases.

4.4.3 A Problem for Everyone

Despite this problem, I think Comesaña is onto something important. Comesaña is right that any adequate theory of justification needs to explain the difference between doxastic justification and propositional justification. Moreover, it does seem that any adequate account of this distinction will have to say something about the *basis* for the agent's belief. Of course, our theorist might not use the language of "basing" explicitly, but they will have to invoke a concept that plays a similar – if not equivalent – role: for example, they will have to talk about the *reasons why* the agent formed their belief, or the *way* the agent formed their belief, or the *manner* or *method* whereby they formed their belief.

---

[47] We already saw a version of this problem with Unknown Symptoms (Section 4.1.3). There, we noted that cases with this structure pose a problem for Reliabilist Support. The present point is that they also pose a problem for Comesaña's solution to the generality problem.

To see this point, go back to our pal Poirot, who believes the groundskeeper is guilty. Why isn't Poirot's belief doxastically justified? The obvious answer: because his belief was formed by consulting a ouija board. Here this phrase, "formed by consulting a ouija board" specifies the basis for his belief (or, if one prefers, the *way* or *method* or *process* by which he formed it).

I argued earlier that appealing to the basis for a belief does not solve the Generality Problem; it just reintroduces it under a new guise, because there will be indefinitely many ways of individuating the basis for a given belief. In Smith's Vision, what is the basis for Smith's belief in MAPLE? Is it one of E1 ... E7? Is it E_{token}? Something else? The same questions arise if rather than using the language of basing, we talk about the *way* or *method* Smith formed her belief.

This suggests that Comesaña was right that everyone faces a version of the Generality Problem. But he was wrong in thinking that the solution is to import the evidentialist's account of doxastic justification into the process reliabilist camp. Rather, the Generality Problem remains a problem for everyone, evidentialists included. Saying this does not amount to giving a solution to the Generality Problem (though this point is certainly compatible with the solutions canvassed in Section 3). But it does show that the Generality Problem is not restricted to reliabilism.[48,49]

4.5 Taking Stock

This short section explored some recent proposals for synthesizing reliabilism and evidentialism. The idea of bringing evidentialist elements into reliabilism holds significant promise for assuaging reliabilism's headaches. However, the most straightforward attempts to fulfill this promise yield more headaches. Summarizing:

(i) The most straightforward synthesis strategies involve injecting evidential notions – in particular, evidence possession and evidential support – into a reliabilist framework. But this raises a question of how to unpack these notions. Can they be explained in non-epistemic terms?

(ii) One strategy for handling the cases of Norman and Truetemp is to deny that they have any evidence in favor of their beliefs. But we can imagine versions of the cases where these agents do have some distinctive mental

---

[48] The idea that everyone faces a version of the Generality Problem and so it is not a *distinctive* problem for reliabilists is sometimes known as a "parrying response." For discussion, see Bishop (2010), Matheson (2015), and Tolly (2017).

[49] In Section 1.3, we noted that many truth-tracking theories of knowledge (such as sensitivity and safety-based theories) relativize knowledge to belief-forming methods. A version of the Generality Problem arises for these accounts as well.

states associated with their belief-forming processes. Why don't these states count as evidence?

(iii) Are we simply adding an extra evidentialist condition onto a reliabilist substructure? If so, there is a risk that the theory becomes disunified. Those attracted to reliabilism will want to justify any evidential condition in reliabilist terms, in particular, in terms of the goal of reliably attaining the truth.

(iv) One motivation for introducing an evidential element into reliabilism is to solve the Generality Problem. But there is reason to think that the resulting solution is inadequate, since it faces a "revenge" version of the Generality Problem.

5 Toward a More Promising Reliabilist Epistemology

5.1 An Impasse and the Path Ahead

In the last section we reached an impasse. To recap: An attractive strategy for rescuing reliabilism is to inject evidentialist elements into the theory. But doing so risks abandoning the features that made reliabilism attractive in the first place. Moreover, the main reliabilist-evidentialist syntheses that have been defended in the literature fail to fully solve the problems they were trying to fix.

This section explores how we might move beyond this impasse. As before, the general strategy is to incorporate evidential notions into a reliabilist framework. But rather than taking these evidential notions as primitive, we give them a further elucidation and justification in naturalistic, and specifically reliabilist-friendly, terms. Call a hybrid theory "reductive" if it takes this form.

I'll sketch two strategies for developing a reductive hybrid view. The first makes use of a reasons-based architecture for theorizing about justification. But it goes on to explain the notion of a possessed reason in reliabilist terms, identifying an agent's reasons for believing something with the inputs to their reliable belief-forming processes. The second strategy explains justification using evidential probabilities. But it goes on to explain these evidential probabilities in terms of justified credences, which are explained in terms of reliability.

These two reductive approaches rely on different theoretical frameworks; I'll discuss some of the tradeoffs along the way. But they share important commonalities. Unlike traditional reliabilism, both make the justificatory status of a belief depend on an agent's *total* evidence or epistemic reasons. In this regard, they both accept a version of the Total Evidence Requirement. And, unlike the hybrid views discussed in the last section, they are both committed to explaining these evidentialist notions in terms of reliability.

5.2 Reasons Reliabilism

5.2.1 Reliable Reasons

The key explanatory notion for process reliabilists is a *reliable process*. A process is a function from input states of the agent to doxastic states (Section 1). This suggests one way of explaining evidence in reliabilist terms. We could identify an agent's possessed evidence with the *inputs* to their reliable processes.

In Beddor (2021), I offered one way fleshing this out. A terminological preliminary: My 2021 treatment was formulated in terms of an agent's *reasons*, rather than their *evidence*, and the present exposition will follow suit in this regard. This difference is arguably terminological. After all, the concepts, "evidence" and "reasons" are arguably interchangeable, at least when the reasons in question are epistemic reasons to believe.

On to the details. Following Beddor (2021), we could formulate a reliabilist account of reasons recursively. The base clause specifies an agent's *basic* or *non-inferential* reasons for belief – that is, reasons that do not depend on any further beliefs:

> *Reliable Reasons (Base Clause)* If s is a non-doxastic state of an agent A, and there is a reliable process available to A which, when given s as input, is disposed to produce a belief in p, then A has a prima facie reason to believe p.

As with ARP, this account invokes the notion of an 'available' belief-forming process. As we noted in our discussion of ARP, one option would be to define availability in terms of *ability*: A process is available to an agent, in the relevant sense, provided the agent has the ability to use that process.[50]

To illustrate the view, suppose you see the sun setting on the horizon. This perceptual experience is a non-doxastic state (it is not a belief). If you're like most people, you have some process available to you that, given this perceptual experience, is disposed to produce a belief that the sun is setting. This process is generally reliable. (Of course, the exact description of this process will depend on one's solution to the Generality Problem. But most solutions to the Generality Problem will agree that you have such a reliable process available to you; they'll just disagree on the details of how to characterize it.) Given this, the Base Clause predicts that you have a prima facie reason to believe the sun is setting.

---

[50] Cf. Lasonen-Aarnio (forthcoming) on "feasible" dispositions.

The recursive clause of the definition gives an account of an agent's non-basic or inferential reasons for belief:

> *Reliable Reasons (Recursive Clause)* If A has a prima facie reason to believe p, and there is some conditionally reliable process available to A which, when given a belief in p as input, is disposed to produce a belief in q, then A has a prima facie reason for A to believe q.

To illustrate with the sunset example, suppose you believe the sun is setting (based on your perceptual experience), and from this you infer that night will soon fall. Your inferential process is conditionally reliable: If the sun is setting, then in most circumstances night will soon fall. So the Recursive Clause predicts that you have a prima facie reason to believe that night will soon fall.

Add the customary closure clause (A does not have any other prima facie reasons for belief), and you have a complete reliabilist theory of reasons.

5.2.2 Reasons, Justification, and Defeat

How does this reliabilist account of reasons relate to justification? One option is to combine Reliable Reasons with a reasons-based account of justification:

> *Reasons Account of Justified Belief:* A's belief that p is:
> (i) prima facie justified iff A's belief that p is based on a prima facie reason (or reasons) to believe p; and
> (ii) ultima facie justified iff A's belief that p is prima facie justified, and the reasons on which it is based are ultimately undefeated.

A reasons-based account of justification has been defended by many philosophers (see esp. Pollock 1987, 1994, 1995). Most of these philosophers (esp. Pollock) were staunch internalists. But this is a choice point; there is nothing in the abstract structure of the Reasons Account of Justified Belief that forces internalism upon us. Consequently, those who feel the pull of reliabilism's explanatory advantages are welcome to take this account on board, combining it with Reliable Reasons. Call the resulting combination, "Reasons Reliabilism."[51]

As it stands, however, the resulting theory is incomplete. The ultima facie justification clause (clause (ii)) relies on the notion of being *ultimately undefeated*. How should we unpack this notion?

Here too, we can take a cue from reasons-based approaches. Pollock develops a view on which there are two types of defeaters, both of which can be specified

---

[51] See also Graham and Lyons (2021), which also explores the prospects of integrating reliabilism with Pollock's framework.

in terms of reasons. A rebutting defeater for a belief B is a prima facie reason to think B is false. An undercutting defeater for B is a prima facie reason to think that one's reasons for B are not suitably connected to the truth. There are different ways of spelling out what counts as a "suitable connection" here. But for reliabilists, it's natural to spell this out in terms of reliability. That is:

> *Defeat:* A's *prima facie* reason r for believing p is defeated iff:
> (i) A has a rebutting defeater for r – i.e., A has a prima facie reason to believe p is false, or
> (ii) A has an undercutting defeater for r – i.e., A has a prima facie reason to believe that A's prima facie reasons for believing p do not indicate the truth of p.[52]

Clause (ii) of the Reasons Account of Justification invoked "ultimately undefeated" arguments. At first glance, it might be tempting to say that A's reasons for belief are ultimately undefeated if and only if A does not have a defeater for these reasons. But such an account would flounder on defeater defeat. Recall Double Testimony: Dina has the perceptual experience of a red sculpture; Steph tells her it is illuminated by a red light; then Cora tells her that Steph is mistaking this sculpture for another. In this scenario, Dina has a defeater for her reasons for believing the sculpture is red. But since this reason is itself defeated, we want to say that Dina's belief is ultima facie justified.

In light of this issue, Pollock opts for a more complicated way of computing the justificatory status of a belief. His account evolved over the course of his work, but to give a general flavor for the approach, it will suffice to sketch his early (1987) treatment. Pollock introduces a technical notion of being *in at a level*, which is defined recursively. Every reason for holding a belief is in at level 0. This corresponds to the idea that every reason confers prima facie justification on a belief. A reason r is in at level $n+1$ iff r is not defeated by any reason that is in at level n; otherwise, it is out at level $n+1$. Pollock proposes:

> *Ultimately Undefeated Reasons:* An agent's *prima facie* reason r is ultimately undefeated iff there is a level m such that, for every level $n \geq m$, r is in at level n.

To see the whole theory in action, start with a simple case of defeat, such as Seeing Red. According to Reliable Reasons, Dina's perceptual experience of

---

[52] There are two ways that this might happen. One way would be for A to acquire a reason for thinking that their prima facie reasons in support of p are not in general the kind of things that would serve as reliable indicators of the the truth of p-related matters (e.g., you learn that your eyesight is very poor, and hence your perceptual experiences do not reliably indicate the truth of what they purport to represent). The other way would be for A to acquire a reason for thinking that their prima facie reasons in support of p do not indicate the truth of p on this particular occasion (e.g., you learn that the lighting in this particular room is deceptive).

a red-looking sculpture is a prima facie reason to believe that there is a red sculpture in front of her, since there is a generally reliable process that takes her from an experience of this sort to a belief in its content. This reason is in at level 0 (since every reason is in at level 0). But Steph's testimony provides an undercutting defeater for this reason. After all, there is some reliable process available to Dina which, when fed Steph's testimony as input, is disposed to produce a belief in its content.[53] So Reliable Reasons predicts that Dina has a prima facie reason to believe that the sculpture is illuminated by red lights, and hence that her perceptual experience does not reliably indicate the color of the sculpture. Moreover, in the original Seeing Red case, the defeater provided by Steph's testimony is not defeated. So the reason provided by Steph's testimony is in at every level, and the reason provided by Dina's visual experience is out at every level ≥ 1. Consequently, the reason provided by Steph's testimony is ultimately undefeated, and the reason provided by Dina's perceptual experience is ultimately defeated. So Dina's belief is prima facie justified, but not ultima facie justified.

To see how the account handles defeater defeat, let's walk through Double Testimony. The analysis works much as before, except in this case Steph's testimony is defeated by Cora's testimony. Since Cora's testimony lacks a defeater, it is in at every level. So the reason provided by Steph's testimony is out at every level ≥ 1. Consequently, the reason provided by Dina's perceptual experience is out at level 1 (since it is defeated by a reason that is in at level 0 – namely, Steph's testimony), but it is in at level 2 (since it has no defeater that is in at level 1 or above), and it is also in at every level thereafter. Consequently, the view predicts that the reason provided by Dina's perceptual experience is ultimately undefeated, and hence her belief is ultima facie justified.

5.2.3 Problems Solved?

Reductive and explanatory. Recall our impasse for reliabilist-evidentialist hybrids. These accounts inject evidentialist elements into reliabilism, elements such as *evidence possession* and *evidential support*. They thus incur a commitment to provide an account of these evidentialist notions – an account that remains faithful to reliabilism's reductive promise. The hybrid theories discussed in Section 4 struggled to fulfill this commitment.

---

[53] Here too, the exact description of the process will hinge on our solution to the Generality Problem. But most reliabilists will want to allow that testimony provides justification. So most will allow that there is a reliable process such as *believing the testimony of others* or *believing what seemingly reliable people tell you* available to Dina, even if they disagree on the exact description of this process.

Reasons Reliabilism fares better. It takes on board two key elements from a reasons-y version of evidentialism: the notion of a prima facie reason to believe something, and the notion of a defeater. However, if we follow Pollock in defining defeaters in terms of prima facie reasons, there is really just one evidentialist concept: the concept of a prima facie reason for belief. Reliable Reasons then explains this concept in reliabilist terms: prima facie reasons for belief are just the inputs to reliable or conditionally reliable processes.

Defeat. Reasons Reliabilism also offers to make progress on reliabilism's problems with defeat. Simple Process Reliabilism yields the wrong verdicts in even simple cases of defeat, such as Seeing Red. Pollock's reasons-based framework was designed to account for the full range of cases of defeat. Reasons Reliabilism helps itself to this basic model for explaining defeat; it just goes on to analyze the fundamental concepts in reliabilist terms. Our discussion in Section 5.2.2 illustrates how the account delivers the right results about simple cases, such as Seeing Red, as well as more complex cases of defeater defeat, for example, Double Testimony. This last point marks an advantage over the ARP, which gives the right result in Seeing Red, but flounders on defeater defeat.

We saw in Section 3 that ARP also gave the wrong results in cases like Thinking About Unger. Reasons Reliabilism avoids this problem. If Harry were to use his Unger Predictor, he would abandon his belief that there is a tree in front of him. But, crucially, the output of his Unger Predictor is not a belief that there is not a tree in front of him, or a belief that his current experiences do not reliably indicate whether there is a tree before him. So Reasons Reliabilism says that he does not have a defeater for his belief that there is a tree in front of him.[54]

---

[54] As noted in Section 3 (fn.38), Beddor (2015a) also offers a counterexample to the necessity of ARP. In this case, Clarence reliably forms a belief that p. A reliable informant subsequently tells Clarence $\sim p$. But Clarence irrationally disbelieves everything this informant says. Intuitively, Clarence's belief is defeated. Some might wonder: isn't this case also a problem for Reasons Reliabilism? However, I think Reasons Reliabilism has the resources for handling this case. If we define availability in terms of ability, the key question is whether Clarence has the ability to believe his informant's testimony. If the answer is *no*, then it seems to me we should question the verdict that his belief is defeated. After all, if he is truly incapable of responding to some testimony, then it does not seem that he ought to revise his belief in response to that testimony (due to ought-implies-can considerations). Suppose, then, that he does have the ability to heed his interlocutor's testimony, but this ability is *masked* by his irrational mistrust. Then Reasons Reliabilism predicts Clarence does have a *prima facie* reason to believe p is false. Since this reason is not defeated, his belief in p is defeated. (This highlights one advantage of formulating the account in terms of dispositions, rather than counterfactuals.)

Norman & Co. Does Reasons Reliabilism also help with Norman and Truetemp? One option would be to appeal to Goldman's suggestion that Norman and Truetemp are cases of defeat. Recall Goldman's proposal that Norman should reason along the following lines: "If I had a reliable clairvoyant ability, I probably would have gotten some evidence of this by now. So I probably don't have a reliable clairvoyant ability." As we noted in Section 3, this diagnosis seems plausible; however, we lacked a reliabilist account of defeat to substantiate it.

Reasons Reliabilism offers one way of filling this gap. Presumably, Norman has some state that serves as the input to his clairvoyance. This might be a mental state with its own distinctive phenomenology, or it might be some input that lacks any qualia. Either way, Reliable Reasons says that Norman has a prima facie reason to believe the President is in NY. But now consider all of Norman's experiences which suggest that he lacks a reliable clairvoyant ability. These would include the absence of any experience of uncovering any indication of his clairvoyant abilities. They would also include any general experiences suggesting that most people lack any such faculty (e.g., reports of self-proclaimed clairvoyants whose claims did not withstand public scrutiny). Now, there is a reliable process available to Norman that takes all these experiences and beliefs as input and produces as output a belief that he probably does not have reliable clairvoyance. Consequently, these experiences constitute an undercutting defeater for his belief that the President is in NY. Since this undercutting defeater is not itself defeated, he is not ultima facie justified in believing the President is in NY. Similar remarks apply, *mutatis mutandis*, to Truetemp.[55]

5.2.4 Comparisons

Much like traditional reliabilism, Reasons Reliabilism grounds the justificatory status of a belief entirely in facts about the reliability of belief-forming processes. At the same time, the view has a different structure than traditional reliabilism. Rather than simply equating justification with being the output of a reliable process, it takes the justificatory status of a belief to be a complex function of an agent's total prima facie reasons, where these reasons are the

---

[55] What about the case of Nyrmoon (and Noramoon), where arguably intuitions pull in the opposite direction? As noted in Section 3, one option is to argue that the description of Nyrmoon makes it natural to suppose he has gathered some evidence about the track record of his clairvoyance, or at least some evidence that other members of his species have such clairvoyance, even if he hasn't explicitly reflected on this evidence. If this is right, his evidence differs from Norman's. (As noted there, we could also combine the defeater diagnosis with some of the other responses to the clairvoyance problem, such as Normal Worlds Reliabilism or the primal systems view.)

inputs to reliable processes. This holistic sensitivity to an agent's total reasons enables the view to make progress on some of the cases where traditional reliabilism flounders (cases of defeat, as well as Norman and Truetemp). In many of these problem cases, the agent has a reliably formed belief, but they are not appropriately responding to the full set of reasons bearing on their belief.

It is also worth flagging a feature of Reasons Reliabilism that sets it apart from both standard evidentialism and certain hybrid theories. Many evidentialists model evidential support in probabilistic terms: A body evidence e supports believing p if and only if the probability of p, conditional on e, is sufficiently high (Section 2). And at least some hybrid theorists follow suit (Section 4). By contrast, Reasons Reliabilism makes no overt reference to probabilities. Of course, when an agent's beliefs are based on probabilistic reasoning, Reliable Reasons can accommodate such reasoning, provided it is reliable or conditionally reliable. But the notion of evidential reasoning does not play a starring role in its theory of justification.

Is this difference a feature or a bug? This is open for debate. An argument for viewing it as a feature: views that invoke evidential probabilities face the now-familiar question of how to explain evidential probabilities in reliabilist terms. Reasons Reliabilism sidesteps these questions altogether.

An argument for viewing it as a bug: Epistemologists should care about evidential probabilities! And many epistemologists, particularly those of an evidentialist persuasion, have thought these evidential probabilities are closely tied to justification. Moreover, the objection continues, even if we set aside the justificatory status of beliefs, there remains the question of what determines the justificatory status of *degrees of belief* (AKA credences). It seems very plausible that the answer to this question will involve probabilities – a thought that forms the backbone of Bayesian epistemology. If a reliabilist framework downplays or dismisses evidential probabilities, so much the worse for that framework.

There is, I think, some merit in the reply. This motivates considering whether there is a principled way for reliabilists to make sense of justified credence and evidential probabilities. Doing so will have the added advantage of addressing an important lacuna in reliabilist frameworks, which historically have focused on binary belief rather than credence.[56]

5.3 Justified Credence for Reliabilists

5.3.1 Justified Credence

In Section 2, we briefly canvassed some positions on evidential probability. Subjective Bayesians understand evidential support in terms of a subjective

---

[56] Though see Dunn (2015), Tang (2016), and Pettigrew (2021). I discuss some of these proposals next.

probability function c reflecting an agent's credences. According to subjective Bayesians, there are no constraints on c other than the formal synchronic requirements of probabilistic coherence and the diachronic requirement to conditionalize on the evidence. As we saw, this view is too permissive. Someone who begins with a prior credence of 1 in the proposition that we should wear tin hats to protect ourselves from the space invaders in our midst is justified in doing so, by the subjective Bayesian's lights.

This suggests that more is required for epistemically justified credences than satisfying subjective Bayesian strictures. But what more, exactly? This section addresses this question from a broadly reliabilist perspective.

5.3.2 Hypothetical Frequencies

In an important discussion of how to extend reliabilism to credences, Tang (2016) defends a reliabilist view that appeals hypothetical frequencies:

> *Grounds*: An agent A's credence of x in p is justified iff:
>
> (1) It is based on some ground g, where the objective probability (understood as hypothetical relative frequency) of the credence having a true content given that it is based on g approximates or equals x, and
> (2) There is no more inclusive ground g' had by A such that the objective probability (again, understood as hypothetical relative frequency) having a true content given that it is based on g' neither approximates nor equals x.[57]

This is an elegant view, faithful to reliabilism's naturalistic ambitions. It also bears an interesting resemblance to some of the views discussed in Section 4. Note that clause (1) of Grounds encodes a version of the Evidential Basing Requirement, where "evidence" has been swapped with "grounds," and where evidential support is understood in terms of objective probability, similar to Reliabilist Support. So we might wonder: Do the challenges for the Evidential Basing Requirement arise here as well? Take Norman. Suppose Norman has a credence of .9 that the president is in NY, and the ground for this credence is the mental experience produced by his clairvoyance, CLAIR(*PRES, NY*). As we noted in Section 4, the objective probability (understood as hypothetical relative frequency) of his credence having a true content, given that it is based on CLAIR(*PRES,NY*), could be high – it might also be .9. Or take Unknown Symptoms, where a doctor in training is diagnosing a patient based on their symptoms. Suppose they have a credence of x that the patient has condition C,

---

[57] Tang's view takes inspiration from Alston's indicator reliabilism (1988, 2005). See Pettigrew 2018 for a closely related view.

based on symptoms S. As a matter of fact, the objective probability that the patient has C, given that they display symptoms S, is x. But it seems it could still be a fluke that our aspiring doctor's credence matches the objective probabilities (suppose that they have not researched whether there are alternative possible causes of this constellation of symptoms).[58]

5.3.3 From Truth to Accuracy

Let's try a different tack. Recall that the key idea behind process reliabilism is that beliefs are justified if they are formed by a truth-conducive process. What would an analogous view of justified credence look like?

When it comes to credences, talk of truth or falsity seems out of place: It seems odd to describe a .7 credence that it will rain as true if it rains and false otherwise. But it does seem that a .7 credence in a true proposition is more accurate than a .2 credence in a true proposition. We can think of the accuracy of a credence as its "distance" from the truth: The closer a credence in p is to the truth-value of p (1 if p is true, 0 if p is false), the more accurate that credence in p is. In the formal epistemology literature, a number of "scoring rules" have been proposed for measuring the distance between a credence and the truth,[59] though for our purposes we need not wade into the details of these different accuracy scores. Instead, I want to focus on the underlying idea that there is a close connection between truth and accuracy: Accuracy is the natural analogue – or really generalization of – truth, one that applies to credences.

Taking this connection seriously suggests a promising approach. We could extend a reliabilist account of justified belief to justified credence, by swapping out "belief" with "credence" and "truth" with "accuracy."

5.3.4 Credal Reliabilism (First Pass)

To see this idea in its simplest form, let's start by considering how to generalize Simple Process Reliabilism to credences. Simple Process Reliabilism says that a belief is justified if it is produced by a reliable belief-forming process, where

---

[58] See Comesaña (2018) for a version of this worry. Could one hold that in these examples, clause (1) of Grounds is satisfied but clause (2) is not? This is initially tempting; we've already seen that there is some appeal to regarding Norman as a case of defeat. The problem, however, is that clause (2) models defeat in terms of objective probabilities. Since Norman's total evidence includes CLAIR(*Pres, NY*), which increases the objective probability that the president is in NY to .9, it's not clear why Norman's lack of evidence that he has a reliable clairvoyant faculty should affect this objective probability. Similar remarks apply to Unknown Symptoms.

[59] For example, one prominent scoring rule is the Brier score. The Brier score of an agent's credence c in p is given by the square of the difference between $c(p)$ and the truth-value of (p) – i.e., $(c(p) - T(p))^2$, where $T(p) = 1$ if p is true and 0 otherwise. Lower Brier scores reflect more accurate credences; the Brier score is thus a measure of *in*accuracy.

a belief-producing process is reliable provided it tends to produce true beliefs in some domain of situations D. (As we have seen, there are different candidates for how to characterize this domain: We could identify D with the nearby worlds, or the normal worlds, etc.)

In addition to belief-forming processes, there are *credence-forming* processes, or what I'll call "credal processes" for short. Just as belief-forming processes can be viewed as functions whose inputs are states of agents and whose outputs are beliefs, so too we can view credal processes as functions whose inputs are states of the agent, and whose outputs are credences. Just as we defined a reliable belief-forming process as one that tends to produce true beliefs, we can define a reliable credal process as one that tends to produce accurate credences. We could then propose:

> *Credal Reliabilism (First Pass):* A credence of c in p is justified iff c is produced by a sufficiently reliable credal process – i.e., a credal process that tends to produce sufficiently accurate credences across some domain D.[60]

An approach along these lines closely parallels Simple Process Reliabilism. It just takes the objects of evaluation to be credences rather than beliefs, and takes their success condition to be accuracy rather than truth.

However, as it stands the view does not make any obvious progress on the problems that we sought to solve using a hybrid view. This is unsurprising: Credal Reliabilism (First Pass) is thoroughly reliabilist, offering no concession to evidentialists. For those reliabilists who think that the problems canvassed in Section 3 can be solved without help from evidentialists, this will be no cause for concern. But those attracted to hybrid approaches will naturally wonder whether we can take the view further, by appealing to evidentialist tools. Let's look at how this might go . . .

5.3.5 A Two-Stage Approach

We saw in Section 3 that many process reliabilists (notably Goldman and Lyons) distinguish between beliefs that are produced by a belief-independent process and those that are produced by a belief-dependent process. This distinction bears at least a passing resemblance to the way Bayesian epistemologists think about credences. Bayesians distinguish between (i) the normative constraints on an agent's initial credences – their 'ur-priors', (ii) the normative

---

[60] There are different options for how to cash out the idea of a reliable credence-forming process more precisely. One natural option would be to define the reliability of a credence-producing process as the average accuracy score of the credences it produces across the situations in D where that process is employed.

constraints on an agent's posterior credences, which result from updating their ur-priors as they interact with the world.

Call a credal process "credence-independent" if it does not take any other credences as inputs; call it "credence-dependent" if it does. We could then take the reliability of a credence-dependent process to be some function of the accuracy of the input credences, together with the accuracy of the output credences. There are different options for how to define this function. For example, one option would be to define the degree of reliability of a credence-dependent process as the sum of the accuracy of its input credences and the accuracy of the output credences at every world in the domain. (More on this in Section 5.3.6.)

With these ingredients in place, we could propose a recursive two-stage reliabilist account of justified credences:

Credal Reliabilism (Revised):

(1) If A's credence c in p is an ur-prior, and c was formed via a reliable credence-independent process, then A's credence c in p is justified. (Base Clause)
(2) If A's credence c in p is a posterior credence, and c was formed by applying a sufficiently reliable credence-dependent process to some prior credences, and these prior credences are themselves justified, then A's credence c is justified. (Recursive Clause)
(3) No other credences are justified. (Closure Clause)

This theory is also purely reliabilist: The justificatory status of all credences – both ur-priors and posteriors – is explained in terms of reliability. Where, then, does evidence fit in?

The formal epistemology literature contains various arguments that agents ought to update their prior credences in a particular way: by conditionalizing on their total evidence.[61] One particularly important argument, for our purposes, appeals to the goal of *maximizing accuracy*. If conditionalizing on one's total evidence maximizes accuracy, then evidence may have a place in a reliabilist account of justified credences after all. Specifically, one could try to argue that an agent who conditionalizes on their total evidence is updating their credences in a way that is more reliable than an agent who does not.

---

[61] More precisely, let c_{old} be an agent's prior credence function; let e be their total body of evidence at some later time, and let c_{new} be their posterior credence function at this later time. The requirement to conditionalize says that c_{new} should equal $c_{old}(-|e)$, where $c_{old}(-|e) = c_{old}(- \& e)/c_{old}(e)$ (when defined).

To see how this argument might go, let's take a closer look at one of the accuracy-based arguments for conditionalization, due to Briggs and Pettigrew 2020 (see also Nielsen 2021). Following their terminology, let a *credal strategy* be a two-stage plan. The first is a plan to adopt some prior credence c. The second stage is a *credal act* – a plan for how to update c after gaining some new evidence. Say that a credal strategy <c,a> is *conditionalizing* if and only if a encodes a plan to conditionalize c on the evidence the agent subsequently receives.

Next, Briggs and Pettigrew propose to extend the notion of accuracy from credences to credal strategies. They show that, given certain constraints on how to score a credal strategy for accuracy:

> *Conditionalization Accuracy-Dominates*: For any credal strategy s that is not conditionalizing, there is some credal strategy s' that is conditionalizing that is guaranteed to be more accurate than s no matter what the world is like.

This result offers one path toward underwriting the idea that conditionalizing on one's total evidence maximizes accuracy.

Let's tie this back to Credal Reliabilism. There is a close parallel between credal strategies and credence-dependent credal processes. So we can extend Briggs and Pettigrew's conceptual framework from the former to the latter. Say that a credence-dependent process is *conditionalizing* iff yields the same posterior credence as conditionalizing on your evidence would.[62] We could then appeal to Conditionalization Accuracy-Dominates to argue for:

> *Conditionalization & Reliability:* A credence-dependent credal process is only *maximally* reliable if it is conditionalizing.

Some might worry that this way of yoking Credal Reliabilism to evidentialist ideas imposes implausible constraints on how we type credal processes. Specifically, it might seem that the foregoing discussion assumes that *updating by conditionalization on one's total evidence* is a legitimate way of typing credal processes – an assumption that might not be borne out by our preferred solution to the Generality Problem. However, I think we can formulate the proposal in a way that avoids this assumption. The claim is not that *updating by conditionalization on one's total evidence* is a genuine credal process. Rather, the claim is that a credal process is maximally reliable only if it agrees with conditionalization: that is, it yields the same output that the conditionalizing on one's total

---

[62] Formally, let $c_{X(s_1 \ldots s_n)}$ be the posterior credence that results from applying a credence-dependent credal process X to prior credence c, together with certain other input states of the agents $s_1 \ldots s_n$. Let c_e be the posterior credence function that results from conditionalizing a prior credence c on the agent's total evidence e. Then a credence-dependent credal process X is conditionalizing iff $c_{X(s_1 \ldots s_n)} = c_e$.

evidence would yield. This claim is noncommittal on how exactly we type credal processes. It is thus compatible with a number of different solutions to the Generality Problem.[63]

5.3.6 Problems Solved?

If an argument along these lines succeeds, we could apply it to defeat. Take Seeing Red. If Dina simply ignores the defeater provided by Steph's testimony, then she is failing to conditionalize on her total evidence. And so her credal process – however exactly we characterize it – is less than maximally reliable.

If we view Norman and Truetemp as cases of defeat, we could tell a similar story. If Norman does not take into account his indirect evidence that he lacks clairvoyance (namely, his lack of evidence that he has clairvoyance), then he is also failing to conditionalize on his total evidence. And so his credal process is also less than maximally reliable.

Let me briefly mention two potential objections to this diagnosis. First, Conditionalization & Reliability says that a credence-dependent credal process is only *maximally* reliable if it is conditionalizing. But Credal Reliabilism (like reliabilism more generally) only requires that an agent uses a *sufficiently* reliable credal process. So even if Dina and Norman are not using maximally reliable credal processes, couldn't their processes still qualify as sufficiently reliable?

We can give this worry more bite. As critics of Bayesianism are fond of pointing out, conditionalization is a complicated and computationally expensive procedure. Very few of us are in practice perfect conditionalizers: We frequently use cognitive heuristics and shortcuts that deviate from conditionalization in certain respects. Even if conditionalization is the reliabilist ideal, presumably many people who fail to reach this ideal can still have justified credences.

While a full treatment of this issue deserves more discussion than I can devote here, let me mention one natural thought. Perhaps a doxastic state (be it a credence or a belief) is justified only if the agent used the most reliable

---

[63] To illustrate this compatibility, consider just one of the solutions to the Generality Problem discussed in Section 3: the Algorithms and Parameters approach. Extended to credences, this approach would hold that the process type relevant to determining the justificatory status of a credence token is given by the complete algorithmic characterization of every psychological process token causally relevant to that credence, together with the associated parameter variables for those processes. Now, given some such complete algorithmic characterization, we can ask whether this algorithm, when relativized to some particular parameters, would yield the token credence as conditionalizing on one's total evidence would in those circumstances. If the answer is *no*, we can appeal to Conditionalization Accuracy-Dominates to argue that this process is less than fully reliable.

process *available* to them which would issue a doxastic state on the topic at hand. (Or one of the most reliable processes available to them, in the case of ties.) As we saw above, we could understand the notion of availability in terms of ability: A process is available to an agent just in case they have the ability to employ it. If critics of Bayesianism are correct that updating by conditionalization exceeds our computational capacities, this shows that no conditionalizing process is genuinely available to us. But even if this is right, most of us do have the ability to adjust our credences in light of our total evidence in a way that at least *roughly approximates* the result of conditionalization. Yet this is not what Dina does in Seeing Red. She does not adjust her beliefs/credences *at all* in light of Steph's testimony; she simply ignores it. Likewise with Norman and Truetemp: They do not adjust their beliefs/credences at all in light of their defeating evidence. Perhaps this is what is driving the intuition that these characters lack justification. It's not just that they fail to use a conditionalizing process. They fail to use anything that remotely approximates a conditionalizing process. Consequently, they fail to use the most reliable credal process available to them.

A second objection concerns the details of the argument for Conditionalization & Reliability. Briggs and Pettigrew's argument that Conditionalization Accuracy-Dominates relies on some specific assumptions about how to score credal strategies for accuracy. For example, they rely on an assumption they call, "Temporal Separability," according to which the accuracy of a credal strategy $<c,a>$ is the sum of accuracy of c, together with the accuracy of the credence that results from updating c on the evidence in accordance with a. So in order to use their result to establish Conditionalization & Reliability, we would need to adopt a corresponding constraint on how to measure the reliability of credence-dependent processes: Specifically, the reliability of a credence-dependent process is the sum of the accuracy of its input credences and the accuracy of its output credences, at every world in the domain. But it's not a priori obvious why we should prefer this measure of reliability to others. For example, an alternative measure would be to define the reliability of a credence-dependent process just in terms of the accuracy of its *output* credences. If we use this 'output' measure instead, we no longer have an argument that conditionalization is guaranteed to be the most reliable credence-dependent process. One question for future exploration is whether we can give principled arguments for preferring one of these measures of reliability over the other.[64]

---

[64] They also rely on the assumption that accuracy is measured using a strictly proper scoring rule, where a scoring rule U is strictly proper iff the expected accuracy of a given credence function Cr, when calculated using U and Cr, is strictly greater than the expected accuracy of any alternative credence function. The usual argument for this assumption is that if our scoring

However, it is worth noting that even if we lack an a priori proof that conditionalization is guaranteed to be the most reliable updating process, no matter what the world is like, all is not lost. It might still turn out that *normally* the most reliable credence-dependent credal process available to an agent is a conditionalizing process (or one that approximates conditionalization).[65] Perhaps this weaker claim is sufficient for the reliabilist's purposes. After all, a key part of the externalist revolution is that justification depends on contingent relations to one's environments – relations that might not be discoverable by a purely a priori argument.

5.3.7 Back to Belief

A final question concerns how this all relates to justified belief. Credal Reliabilism is an account of justified credence. How does this bear on the conditions under which an outright belief is justified?

There are a couple of possibilities. Some philosophers hold that there is a particularly tight connection between belief and credence. According to a view sometimes known as "Lockeanism," all it is to believe p is to have a sufficiently high credence in p. If we accept Lockeanism, then the justificatory status of an agent's credences determines the justificatory status of their beliefs. Alternatively, we might reject Lockeanism but still hold that justified belief requires high evidential probability, which we could then explain in terms of justified credences.

To illustrate, recall the Two Component View from Section 4, which held:

Two Component View (Reprised): A's belief p is justified iff both:

(i) It is produced by a reliable process (perhaps operating on certain evidence as input), and
(ii) A's total evidence supports believing p.

---

rule was not strictly proper, an agent's credences would be self-undermining, in a certain sense: an agent might expect that some other credence function is more accurate than their own. However, this argument carries a strong whiff of internalism: the idea is that we can derive a constraint on accuracy by considering what credences would do best by the agent's own lights. Another question for further exploration is whether we can justify the assumption of strict propriety on externalist grounds.

[65] Do we have any reason to think this? Douven (2013) reports the results of computer simulations comparing the results of updating using conditionalization to updating via inference to the best explanation. Douven found that inference to the best explanation sometimes achieves more accurate results more quickly than conditionalization. However, he also found that conditionalization results in greater average accuracy in the long run, at least when accuracy is calculated using the Brier score. For reliabilists, it's natural to measure the reliability of a credence-dependent credal process in terms of its average accuracy in the long-run. So Douven's results might be thought to provide at least some support to the idea that the most reliable processes will tend to be conditionalizing, even when reliability is measured using the 'output' measure.

In Section 4, we raised the worry that clause (ii) leaves the notion of evidential support unexplained. We could use Credal Reliabilism to fill this gap. Specifically, we could take on board the Probabilistic Account of Belief Support (according to which e supports believing p iff $Pr(p|e)$ is sufficiently high) and then go on to explain evidential probabilities in terms of justified credences, for example:

> *Justified Credence & Evidential Probability:* The evidential probability of p, for an agent A with evidence e, is x iff A is justified in having a credence of x in p.

These evidential probabilities can then be explained in reliabilist terms, courtesy of Credal Reliabilism.

5.4 Taking Stock: Two Reductive Hybrid Theories

One of the main challenges facing hybrid theories is to flesh out their evidentialist commitments in a way that is consistent with the motivations behind reliabilism. This section laid out two different strategies for rising to this challenge. The first took the form of a reasons-based account of justification. But it cashed out the notion of reasons in reliabilist terms: Reasons are the inputs to reliable and conditionally reliable processes. The second strategy took a probabilistic turn, exploring whether we can explain evidential probabilities using reliabilist resources. The idea was to explain evidential probabilities in terms of justified credences, which are analyzed along reliabilist lines.

Which of these reductive strategies should we prefer? The answer will depend, in part, on one's position on broader questions – questions, for example, about the role that probabilities should play in a theory of justification. Those who think that evidential probabilities are central to any adequate account of justification will gravitate toward the second approach (Credal Reliabilism); those who tend to view justification as a matter of weighing competing reasons (reasons which might or might not involve probabilities) will prefer the first (Reasons Reliabilism). These broader questions are not just questions for the reliabilist. They arise for *any* theory of justification. My purpose in this section has not been to provide a definitive answer, but rather to lay out some attractive options, highlighting their advantages and disadvantages, and raising some residual issues along the way.[66]

---

[66] Another difference between these two approaches concerns the defeasibility of evidence/reasons. On standard Bayesian models, if I acquire p as evidence, the probability of p conditional on my total evidence is 1; assuming I update by conditionalization, the evidential probability of p will remain 1 no matter what evidence I receive thereafter. So if the proposition, *I see the sun setting* is part of my evidence at some time, then no matter what counterevidence

One larger take-away from this section is that reliabilism can take many forms. Views that seem, at first blush, anathema to reliabilism – reasons-based accounts of justification and views that emphasize evidential probability – can be given a reliabilist twist.

Conclusion

The current status of reliabilism in the philosophical community is somewhat curious. By any measure, reliabilism is one of the canonical theories of justification, featured in pretty much every epistemology textbook or Theory of Knowledge course. And many philosophers express some sympathy for reliabilism, or at least for externalism more generally. At the same time, I hazard that relatively few philosophers today would unhesitatingly describe themselves as reliabilists. Why not?

I suspect this is largely because reliabilism faces well-known problems (Section 3). In view of these problems, even philosophers who are otherwise attracted to the view might well balk before flying the reliabilist flag. But are these problems truly insurmountable?

I have given some reasons for thinking the answer is *no*. Many of the most pressing problems target very simple forms of reliabilism (e.g., Simple Process Reliabilism). One theme in this Element has been that reliabilism need not take such a crude form. To illustrate this point, I have focused on recent attempts to synthesize reliabilism with its supposed rival, evidentialism (Sections 4 and 5). Admittedly, going hybrid comes with challenges of its own. We saw in Section 4 that the main hybrid views in the literature do not fully solve the problems they were introduced to solve, and they risk abandoning some features that rendered reliabilism appealing in the first place. But in Section 5, I argued that this is a problem of implementation rather than principle. There I sketched two more promising hybrid views. One combines reliabilism with a reasons-first theory of justification; the other explains justification in terms of evidential probabilities, which it then unpacks using reliabilist resources.

Both of these reductive hybrid proposals have a very different *structure* from Simple Process Reliabilism. In particular, both make the justificatory status of a belief sensitive to the agent's *total* body of reasons or evidence, rather than just the process that was causally responsible for the belief. In view of this structural difference, these hybrid views are in a good position to handle some of the main objections to traditional reliabilism (specifically, Norman, Truetemp, and cases

---

I receive at some later time, I remain justified in believing this proposition to the strongest degree possible. By contrast, the reasons-based approach allows that all reasons are defeasible: for any reason *r* I get for believing *p*, I could in theory acquire a rebutting or undercutting defeater for *r*.

of defeat). At the same time, these reductive hybrid views retain the selling points of traditional reliabilism. They explain justification in non-epistemic terms, and they ground justification in the goal of truth attainment.

In view of these virtues, reductive hybrid views strike me as the most promising reliabilist theories currently on offer. Admittedly, reductive hybrid views do not automatically solve every problem for reliabilism. In particular, the New Evil Demon Problem and the Generality Problem still lie in wait. However, we might question whether this is a serious cause for concern. After all, we've seen that there are some promising independent solutions to both the New Evil Demon Problem and the Generality Problem – for example, appealing to normal worlds to solve the former, appealing to cognitive science to solve the latter. While these independent solutions do not follow from reductive hybrid views, they are certainly compatible with them. Furthermore, we've seen that the New Evil Demon Problem and the Generality Problem do not merely afflict reliabilism. The former arises for any externalist theory of justification, and hence for any theory that comes with the externalist anti-skeptical strategy that was one of reliabilism's selling points (Section 2). And the Generality Problem afflicts an even wider class of theories (Section 4): It arises for any theory that properly distinguishes between doxastic and propositional justification, which is every adequate theory! Consequently, we saw reason to agree with Comesaña's claim that the Generality Problem is *everyone*'s problem.

Reliabilism is a protean view, which can be embedded in a variety of sophisticated frameworks. Some of these sophisticated frameworks make significant progress on the various problems afflicting simpler – and more familiar – versions of reliabilism. Moreover, there is reason to hope that the remaining problems are tractable. This should come as welcome news to the epistemologist who feels the allure of reliabilism, but hesitates to embrace the view in light of its well-known challenges.

References

Alston, William, 1988, "An Internalist Externalism," *Synthese*, 74: 265–283.
  2005, *Beyond "Justification": Dimensions of Epistemic Evaluation*, Ithaca: Cornell University Press.
  1995, "How to Think about Reliability," *Philosophical Topics*, 23(1): 1–29.
Armstrong, David M., 1973, *Belief, Truth and Knowledge*, Cambridge: Cambridge University Press.
Becker, Kelly, 2008, "Epistemic Luck and the Generality Problem," *Philosophical Studies*, 139: 353–366.
Beddor, Bob, 2015b, "Evidentialism, Circularity, and Grounding," *Philosophical Studies* 172: 1847–1868.
  2021, "Reasons for Reliabilism," In Jessica Brown and Mona Simion (eds.), *Reasons, Justification, and Defeat*. Oxford: Oxford University Press. pp. 146–176.
  2015a, "Process Reliabilism's Troubles with Defeat," *The Philosophical Quarterly*, 65(259): 145–159.
Beddor, Bob and Carlotta Pavese, 2020, "Modal Virtue Epistemology," *Philosophy and Phenomenological Research*, 101(1): 61–79.
Bedke, Matthew, 2010, "Developmental Process Reliabilism: On Justification, Defeat, and Evidence," *Erkenntnis*, 73(1): 1–17.
Bernecker, Sven, 2008, "Agent Reliabilism and the Problem of Clairvoyance," *Philosophy and Phenomenological Research*, 76(1): 164–172.
Bishop, Michael, 2010, "Why the Generality Problem Is Everybody's Problem," *Philosophical Studies*, 151(2): 285–298.
BonJour, Laurence, 1980, "Externalist Theories of Empirical Knowledge," *Midwest Studies in Philosophy*, 5: 53–73.
Briggs, R. A. and Richard Pettigrew, 2020, "An Accuracy-Dominance Argument for Conditionalization," *Noûs* 54(1): 162–181. https://onlinelibrary.wiley.com/doi/10.1111/nous.12258.
Brown, Jessica and Mona Simion (eds.), 2021, *Reasons, Justification, and Defeat*, Oxford: Oxford University Press.
Burge, Tyler, 2003. "Perceptual Entitlement," *Philosophy and Phenomenological Research*, 67: 503–548.
Burge, Tyler, 2010, *Origins of Objectivity*, Oxford: Oxford University Press.
Chisholm, Roderick, 1942, "The Problem of the Speckled Hen," *Mind*, 51(204): 368–373.

Cohen, Stewart, 2003, "Greco's Agent Reliabilism," *Philosophy and Phenomenological Research*, 66(2): 437–443.

1984, "Justification and Truth," *Philosophical Studies*, 46(3): 279–295.

Collett, Thomas and Paul Graham, 2004, "Animal Navigation: Path Integration, Visual Landmarks, and Cognitive Maps," *Current Biology*, 14: R475–R477.

Comesaña, Juan, 2006, "A Well-Founded Solution to the Generality Problem," *Philosophical Studies*, 129(1): 27–47.

2020, *Being Rational and Being Right*, Oxford: Oxford University Press.

2010, "Evidentialist Reliabilism," *Noûs*, 44(4): 571–600.

2018, "Whither Evidentialist Reliabilism?" In McCain Kevin (ed.), *Believing in Accordance with the Evidence: New Essays on Evidentialism*. Cham: Springer, pp. 307–325.

2002, "The Diagonal and the Demon," *Philosophical Studies*, 110(3): 249–266.

Conee, Earl and Richard Feldman, 2004, *Evidentialism: Essays in Epistemology*, Oxford: Oxford University Press.

2008, "Evidence," In Quentin Smith (ed.), *Epistemology: New Essays*, New York: Oxford University Press, 83–104.

1998, "The Generality Problem for Reliabilism," *Philosophical Studies*, 89(1): 1–29.

Douven, Igor, 2013, "Inference to the Best Explanation, Dutch Books, and Inaccuracy Minimization," *The Philosophical Quarterly*, 63(252): 428–444.

Dretske, Fred, 1981, *Knowledge and the Flow of Information*, Cambridge, MA: MIT Press.

Dunn, Jeff, 2015, "Reliability for Degrees of Belief," *Philosophical Studies*, 172(7): 1929–1952.

Feldman, Richard, 2002, *Epistemology*, 1st ed. Boston: Pearson.

Feldman, Richard and Earl Conee, 2001, "Internalism Defended." *American Philosophical Quarterly*, 38(1):1–18.

1988, "Having Evidence," In D. F. Austin (ed.), *Essays Presented to Edmund Gettier*, Dordrecht: Kluwer Academic Publishers, pp. 88–104.

Fodor, Jerry, 1983, *Modularity of Mind*, Cambridge, MA: MIT Press.

Fricker, Elizabeth, 2016, "Unreliable Testimony," In McLaughlin, Brian P., and Kornblith, Hilary (eds.), *Goldman and His Critics*, Malden, MA: Wiley-Blackwell, pp. 88–120.

Fumerton, Richard, 1988, "Foundationalism, Conceptual Regress, and Reliabilism," *Analysis*, 48(4): 178–184.

Gallistel, Charles R., 2007, "Dead Reckoning, Cognitive Maps, Animal Navigation and the Representation of Space: An Introduction," In Margaret E. Jeffries and Wai-Kiang Yeap (eds.), *Robotics and Cognitive Approaches to Spatial Mapping*, Springer Tracts in Advanced Robotics, Vol 38. Berlin, Heidelberg: Springer.

Ghijsen, Harmen, 2016, "Norman and Truetemp Revisited Reliabilistically: A Proper Functionalist Defeat Account of Clairvoyance," *Episteme*, 13(1): 89–110.

Goldman, Alvin, 1967, "A Causal Theory of Knowing," *The Journal of Philosophy*, 64(12): 357–372.

1979 [2012], "What Is Justified Belief?" In George S. Pappas (ed.), *Justification and Knowledge: New Studies in Epistemology*, Dordrecht: Reidel, pp. 1–25; reprinted in his *Reliabilism and Contemporary Epistemology*, New York: Oxford University Press, 2012, pp. 29–49.

1986, *Epistemology and Cognition*, Cambridge, MA: Harvard University Press.

1992, "Epistemic Folkways and Scientific Epistemology," In his *Liaisons: Philosophy Meets the Cognitive and Social Sciences*, Cambridge, MA: MIT Press, pp. 155–175.

2009, "Williamson on Knowledge and Evidence," In Duncan Pritchard and Patrick Greenough (eds.), *Williamson on Knowledge*, Oxford: Oxford University Press. pp. 73–91.

2011a, "Toward a Synthesis of Reliabilism and Evidentialism," In Dougherty (ed.), *Evidentialism and Its Discontents*, New York: Oxford University Press, pp. 254–290.

2011b, "Commentary on Jack Lyons' *Perception and Basic Beliefs*," *Philosophical Studies*, 153: 457–466.

Goldman, Alvin and Bob Beddor, 2021, "Reliabilist Epistemology," In Edward N. Zalta (ed.), *Stanford Encyclopedia of Philosophy*. https://plato.stanford.edu/archives/sum2021/entries/reliabilism/.

Goodman, Jeremy and Bernhard Salow, 2018, "Taking a Chance on KK," *Philosophical Studies*, 175(1): 183–196.

Graham, Peter, 2012, "Epistemic Entitlement," *Noûs*, 46(3): 449–482.

2017, "Normal Circumstances Reliabilism," *Philosophical Topics*, 45(1): 33–61.

2011, "Perceptual Entitlement and Basic Beliefs," *Philosophical Studies*, 153: 467–475.

forthcoming, "The New Evil Demon Problem at 40," *Philosophy and Phenomenological Research*.

References

Graham, Peter and Jack Lyons, 2021, "The Structure of Defeat: Pollock's Evidentialism, Lackey's Framework, and the Prospects for Reliabilism," In Jessica Brown and Mona Simion (eds.), *Reasons, Justification, and Defeat*. Oxford: Oxford University Press. pp. 146–176.

Greco, Daniel, 2014, "Could KK Be OK?" *Journal of Philosophy*, 111(4): 169–197.

2013, "Prodigality and Probability," *Oxford Studies in Epistemology*, 4: 82–107.

Greco, John, 1999, "Agent Reliabilism," *Philosophical Perspectives*, 13: 273–296.

2003, "Further Thoughts on Agent Reliabilism: Replies to Cohen, Geivett, Kvanvig, and Schmitt and Lahroodi," *Philosophy and Phenomenological Research*, 66(2): 466–480.

2000, *Putting Skeptics in Their Place: The Nature of Skeptical Arguments and Their Role in Philosophical Inquiry*, New York: Cambridge University Press.

Grice, Herbert Paul, 1961, "The Causal Theory of Perception," *Proceedings of the Aristotelian Society*, Supp. Vol. xxxv: 121–153.

Grundmann, Thomas, 2009, "Reliabilism and the Problem of Defeaters," *Grazer Philosophische Studien*, 79(1): 65–76.

Hedden, Brian, 2015, "Time-Slice Rationality," *Mind*, 124(494): 449–491.

Jönsson, Martin L., 2013, "A Reliabilism Built on Cognitive Convergence: An Empirically Grounded Solution to the Generality Problem," *Episteme*, 10(3): 241–268.

Kelp, Christoph, 2019, "How to Be a Reliabilist," *Philosophy and Phenomenological Research*, 98: 346–374.

2016, "Justified Belief: Knowledge First-Style," *Philosophy and Phenomenological Research*, 93: 79–100.

Kornblith, Hilary, 2002, *Knowledge and its Place in Nature*, Oxford: Oxford University Press.

Lasonen-Aarnio, Maria, forthcoming, *The Good, Bad, and the Feasible: Knowledge and Reasonable Belief*, Oxford: Oxford University Press.

2010, "Unreasonable Knowledge," *Philosophical Perspectives*, 24: 1–21.

Lehrer, Keith. 1990, *Theory of Knowledge*, London: Routledge.

Lewis, David, 1996, "Elusive Knowledge," *Australasian Journal of Philosophy*, 74(4): 549–567.

Loughrist, Tim, 2021, "Defeaters and the Generality Problem," *Synthese*, 199(5): 13845–13860.

Lyons, Jack C., 2019, "Algorithm and Parameters: Solving the Generality Problem for Reliabilism," *The Philosophical Review*, 128(4): 463–509.

2009, *Perception and Basic Beliefs: Zombies, Modules and the Problem of the External World*, Oxford: Oxford University Press.

2013, "Should Reliabilists Be Worried about Demon Worlds?" *Philosophy and Phenomenological Research*, 86(1): 1–40.

Maier, John and Sophie Kikkert, 2025, "Abilities," In Edward N. Zalta and Uri Nodelman (eds.), *The Stanford Encyclopedia of Philosophy* (Summer 2025 Edition), https://plato.stanford.edu/archives/sum2025/entries/abilities/.

Matheson, Jonathan, 2015, "Is There a Well-Founded Solution to the Generality Problem?," *Philosophical Studies*, 172(2): 459–468.

McCain, Kevin, 2014, *Evidentialism and Epistemic Justification*, New York: Routledge.

Miller, Emelia, 2019, "Liars, Tigers, and Bearers of Bad News, Oh My!: Towards a Reasons Account of Defeat," *The Philosophical Quarterly*, 69(274): 82–99.

Moss, Sarah, 2015, "Time-Slice Epistemology and Action under Indeterminacy," *Oxford Studies in Epistemology*, 5: 172–194.

Nagel, Jennifer, 2021, "Losing Knowledge by Thinking about Thinking," In Jessica Brown and Mona Simion (eds.), *Reasons, Justification, and Defeat*. Oxford: Oxford University Press. pp. 146–176.

Nielsen, Michael, 2021, "Accuracy-Dominance and Conditionalization," *Philosophical Studies*, 178(10): 3217–3236.

Nozick, Robert, 1981, *Philosophical Explanations*, Cambridge, MA: Harvard University Press.

Olsson, Erik, 2016, "A Naturalistic Approach to the Generality Problem," In Brian P. McLaughlin and Hilary Kornblith (eds.), pp. 178–199.

Petersen, Mary and Gillian Rhodes (eds.), 2003, *Perception of Faces, Objects, and Scenes: Analytic and Holistic Processes*, Oxford: Oxford University Press.

Pettigrew, Richard, 2021, "What Is Justified Credence?" *Episteme*, 18(1): 16–30.

Podgorski, Abelard, 2017, "Rational Delay," *Philosophers' Imprint*, 17(5): 1–19.

Pollock, John, 1995, *Cognitive Carpentry*, Cambridge, MA: MIT Press.

1987, "Defeasible Reasoning," *Cognitive Science*, 11: 481–518.

1994, "Justification and Defeat," *Artificial Intelligence*, 67: 377–408.

Pollock, John and Joseph Cruz, 1999, *Contemporary Theories of Knowledge*, Rowman and Littlefield.

Pritchard, Duncan, 2005, *Epistemic Luck*, Oxford: Oxford University Press.

Ramsey, Frank Plumpton, 1931, "Knowledge," In Richard Bevan Braithwaite (ed.), *Foundations of Mathematics and Other Logical Essays*, London: Kegan Paul, pp. 126–128.

Rosch, Eleanor, Carolyn B Mervis, Wayne D Gray, David M Johnson, and Penny Boyes-Braem, 1976, "Basic Objects in Natural Categories," *Cognitive Psychology*, 8(3): 382–439.

Schechter, Joshua, 2017, "No Need for Excuses: Against Knowledge-First Epistemology and the Knowledge Norm of Assertion," In Gordon Carter and Jarvis (eds.), *Knowledge-First: Approaches in Epistemology and Mind*. Oxford: Oxford University Press.

Schroeder, Mark, 2011, "What Does it Take to 'Have' a Reason?" In Andrew Reisner and Asbjørn Steglich-Peterson (eds.), *Reasons for Belief*, New York: Cambridge University Press, pp. 201–222.

Schwitzgebel, Eric, 2008, "The Unreliability of Naïve Introspection," *Philosophical Review*, 117(2): 245–273.

Simion, Mona, 2019, "Knowledge-First Functionalism," *Philosophical Issues*, 29(1): 254–267.

Smithies, Declan, 2014, "The Phenomenal Basis for Epistemic Justification," In Mark Sprevak and Jesper Kallestrup (eds.), *New Waves in Philosophy of Mind*, London: Palgrave-Macmillan. pp. 98–124.

Sosa, Ernest, 1999, "How to Defeat Opposition to Moore," *Philosophical Perspectives*, 13: 137–149.

1993, "Proper Functionalism and Virtue Epistemology," *Noûs*, 27(1): 51–65.

Sutton, Jonathan, 2007, *Without Justification*, Cambridge, MA: MIT Press.

Tang, Weng Hong, 2016, "Reliability Theories of Justified Credence," *Mind*, 125(497): 63–94.

Tolly, Jeffrey, 2017, "A Defense of Parrying Responses to the Generality Problem," *Philosophical Studies*, 174(8): 1935–1957.

White, Roger, 2006, "Problems for Dogmatism," *Philosophical Studies*, 131(3): 525–557.

Wright, Larry, 1973, "Functions," *The Philosophical Review*, 82(2): 139–168.

Williamson, Timothy, forthcoming, "Justification, Excuses, and Sceptical Scenarios," In Fabian Dorsch and Julien Dutant (eds.), *The New Evil Demon Problem*, Oxford: Oxford University Press.

2000, *Knowledge and Its Limits*, Oxford: Oxford University Press.

In memory of Alvin Goldman

Cambridge Elements

Epistemology

Stephen Hetherington
University of New South Wales, Sydney

Stephen Hetherington is Professor Emeritus of Philosophy at the University of New South Wales, Sydney. He is the author of numerous books, including *Knowledge and the Gettier Problem* (Cambridge University Press, 2016), and *What Is Epistemology?* (Polity, 2019), and is the editor of several others, including *Knowledge in Contemporary Epistemology* (with Markos Valaris: Bloomsbury, 2019), and *What the Ancients Offer to Contemporary Epistemology* (with Nicholas D. Smith: Routledge, 2020). He was the Editor-in-Chief of the Australasian Journal of Philosophy from 2013 until 2022.

About the Series

This Elements series seeks to cover all aspects of a rapidly evolving field, including emerging and evolving topics such as: fallibilism; knowing how; self-knowledge; knowledge of morality; knowledge and injustice; formal epistemology; knowledge and religion; scientific knowledge; collective epistemology; applied epistemology; virtue epistemology; wisdom. The series demonstrates the liveliness and diversity of the field, while also pointing to new areas of investigation.

Cambridge Elements

Epistemology

Elements in the Series

Transcendental Epistemology
Tony Cheng

Knowledge and God
Matthew A. Benton

Knowing What It Is Like
Yuri Cath

Disagreement
Diego E. Machuca

On Believing and Being Convinced
Paul Silva Jr

Knowledge-First Epistemology: A Defence
Mona Simion

Emotional Self-Knowledge: How Affective Skills Reveal Our Values, Goals, Cares and Concerns
Matt Stichter and Ellen Fridland

Deception and Self-Deception: A Unified Account
Vladimir Krstić

The Epistemology of Logic
Ben Martin

The Indispensability of Intuitions
Marc A. Moffett

Aesthetic Knowledge
Jon Robson

Reliabilism and Its Rivals
Bob Beddor

A full series listing is available at: www.cambridge.org/EEPI

Printed by Integrated Books International,
United States of America